your teen-ager and you

ANNA B. MOW

ZONDERVAN PUBLISHING HOUSE
GRAND RAPIDS, MICHIGAN

YOUR TEEN-AGER AND YOU

Library of Congress catalog card number: 67-14103

Unless otherwise specified, Scripture quotations are from The Revised Standard Version of the Bible, copyright 1946 and 1952 by the Division of Christian Education of the National Council of the Churches of Christ, and are used by permission.

Quotations marked *NEB* are from *The New English Bible*, New Testament, © The Delegates of the Oxford University Press and The Syndics of the Cambridge University Press 1961. Reprinted by permission.

Grateful acknowledgement is made to the following for permission to use copyrighted material:

ARTHUR JAMES LTD., Publishers, excerpts from Brother Mandus, *For Women Only*.

CHRISTIAN LIFE PUBLICATIONS, excerpts from S. I. McMillen, "How to Avoid Family Problems," *Christian Life* Magazine, Copyright January, 1966 by Christian Life Publications, Inc., Wheaton, Illinois.

CURTIS BROWN, LTD., lines from Ogden Nash, "I Do, I Will, I Have."

THE PLOUGH PUBLISHING HOUSE, excerpts from Eberhard Arnold, *Love and Marriage in the Spirit*.

THE MACMILLAN COMPANY, quotations from J. B. Phillips, *The New Testament in Modern English*, copyright 1958 by J. B. Phillips.

First printing..........April, 1967
Second printing..........July, 1967
Third printing........October, 1967
Fourth printing...............1968
Fifth printing 1969
Sixth printing 1970
Seventh printing..............1971

DEDICATED

To my Lord
with gratitude for His unmerited love.

To Baxter, my own husband
who has helped me to know the best of human love.

CONTENTS

Preface

I. LOVE CONSIDERED

II. LOVE LIVED

PREFACE

It is easy to be orthodox in a statement of belief. It is even easy to find an arrogant security in the accepted forms of religion, but in moments of honest appraisal the suspicion arises that there is a missing link somewhere. The child who is in the *receiving* state seems to accept what his parents say, but when he reaches the stage of *questioning* adolescence he does not come through to an acceptance of his parents' statement of belief. This distresses his orthodox parents. Then, too, there are the neighbors who do not "believe." Why don't they join in with the church people?

Perhaps Coventry Patmore, the nineteenth-century British poet gave the answer: "God is the only reality, and *we are only real so far as we are in His order, and He is in us.*" If we are not getting results, perhaps we are not truly in God's order. If God is the only reality, then it must be the God of love as revealed in the life of Jesus Christ on earth. If we believe this, isn't it strange that we accept love for our daily living as long as all goes well, but when relationships get difficult we go back to the ways of the world? Christian parents and children, husbands and wives seem to have as much trouble in their relationships as their non-believing neighbors do.

Rufus Mosely said, "The truth is so simple that the wise can't see it." The will of God is the simplest thing a person can do, if he will only choose it — even when, from a human standpoint, it looks impractical. In the long run it is the only thing that works. With a simple faith in God-love we will here consider our family relationships.

Of course, those parents who are happy in their married love do better with their children, but those who have troubled relationships need not despair. In a troubled world they can show their growing, groping, yearning teen-agers the love-way out of difficulties into the maturity of the love God offers to each one of us through Christ.

I am not writing as a "professional" of any kind. But I have learned that it is wise to accept the definition of love that Jesus lived out in all His human relationships. I would count no human relationship as impossible until God-love had been truly tried. The message of this book is as simple as that.

My deepest gratitude again to Genie Price for reading my manuscript and for giving me valuable help in re-writing. And thanks again for the fourth time to Cecile Dowdy for typing the manuscript so the Editor could read it.

Thanks, too, to those who have given me permission to use their stories. I thank God for those who have found that God-love works and that there is hope for even the hopeless.

ANNA B. MOW

Roanoke, Va.

Part One
LOVE CONSIDERED

1

HOW DO YOU LOVE YOUR TEEN-AGER?

Nancy was an authentic "sweet sixteen" — a joy and satisfaction to her mother and a source of justifiable pride to her preacher father. She was the accepted leader of her youth groups at church and in school. No one made her self-conscious of her father's position as religious leader in the far western community. She was proud of him. They were a happy family.

Then Nancy's father was moved to another church in the deep south. The family lost the socially relaxed environment of the far West and found themselves in the provincialism of a new closed community. The closely knit youth group in the new church was slow to accept Nancy with her unaffected western ways. The non-church group appreciated her vivacious beauty and quickly claimed her as one of their own. This made the church group doubly suspicious of her. They were shocked that "their" preacher's daughter would run with "that" crowd. Nancy didn't feel at ease with them either but they alone were kind to her.

Nancy's parents were dismayed. They trusted their daughter but they had the church gossips on their hands. Then the inevitable crisis came. Nancy accepted a date with an undesirable young man who planned to take her to a questionable place. She didn't care about him but she was greatly disconcerted by the change in her church so-

11

cial life, and in defiance she accepted the date. Her frightened mother peremptorily refused to permit her daughter to go.

Her mother's sudden refusal added another element to Nancy's conflict — wasn't she old enough to choose her own friends? Now blind with determination she ran out of the house without a word to her mother. Even though she was barefooted and in shorts she began walking to the city twenty miles away — not thinking, just walking. Her feet began to bleed, each step became agony, so she thumbed a ride. She escaped the hazards of that ride and spent the rest of the night alone in the back seat of a car in a garage parking lot.

Across the chasm of no communication a father and mother paced the night hours away in inexpressible anguish and panic for their only child. The terror of such hours cannot be forgotten. Must the police be called? What does one say to them? What will the church members think? But above all, where is our daughter? How does one pray in such an hour?

Relief, answered prayer, came in the early morning hours. The garage man found her and brought her home. But the heartbreaking question lingered in the mother's heart, "Where did we fail our girl?"

Where did we fail our girl? Our boy? How many parents have agonized over this same question? The question usually comes to honest parents who cannot understand the rebellion of a child, so they add their own frustration to that of the bewildered teen-ager. A frustrated parent cannot help a frustrated adolescent. To be a help, a parent must understand the reasons for rebellion, and he must be able to maintain a relationship of love through whatever comes.

Six-year-old Mary whispered to her Daddy, "Lucy has a boy friend. I saw them kiss and kiss and kiss." Even though Lucy was only thirteen she had a sixteen-year-old girl friend who dated constantly. This father followed the authoritarian pattern of his own father and told Lucy she could not see her girl friend again. Lucy's rebellion filled

12

him with anger. Her refusal to confide in him or her mother filled them both with panic. Nothing resulted but anger, more panic and more rebellion.

Some years ago a distraught mother came with her story of unexpected disaster. This devout woman had been greatly blessed in her service to the church. Even though she was often absent from home she had no special concern because her own mother was there to care for her family. She thought she had every reason to trust her lovely talented daughter. But tragedy slashed across their lives: her daughter was going to have a baby — by a married man. The father insisted on an abortion to protect their prestige in the church and in the community. But the mother and daughter could not face — murder. Neither did they know how to face the inevitable sequel of this predicament.

After some time the mother was able to face the situation realistically and to take the most redemptive way out. She was able to transfer the emphasis from saving of family pride to the salvaging of the best in life still possible for this beautiful girl. Out of a new understanding of God's love a way was found to go through the dark days ahead without shirking any responsibility to the unborn babe who did not ask for life. The painful question in that mother's heart was: "Have the difficulties her father and I have had in our marriage had a harmful influence in our daughter's life?"

Do you love *your* teen-ager that much? A minister and his wife had to find out how much they loved their son. This son questioned his faith in God while he was still in high school. By his second year in college he had discarded it entirely as something naive and prescientific. When he was home on vacation he arrogantly flaunted his new ideas and his new smoking habit before his troubled parents. When his mother asked him not to smoke in the house he accused her of being unloving and he stopped coming home.

The distress of his devout parents at this increasing barrier between them and their son drove them to their knees in a new way. Had they themselves closed doors of communication? This their own son was a stranger to them. How could they understand this stranger and re-establish rapport with him? They could not undo the past, but they could do more to understand him in the future whether he accepted their love or not. They sought for a redemptive way through from *where they were* and found a new faith in the understanding, patient love of God. They accepted the discipline of this love for themselves as parents. They quit confessing their son's sins and eventu-ally their matured God-given love set the son free from his antagonisms toward them. He came home to live while attending a nearby university. He began to treat his par-ents as real persons. He found, too, that he had to get acquainted with them all over again. He was intrigued by the new relationship with them. And his parents prayed that this new relationship with them would be the beginning of a new relationship with God also.

They really loved their son.

It seems to be fashionable to talk about possessive mo thers, domineering fathers and rebellious children, but in spite of all the talk, or even the reason for it, there still are good homes where family relationships are what they ought to be. A college girl raised in the Orient wrote a paragraph or so on her "home letter" every day. Her friends thought it strange that she would hold such a tie with her family. They were all glad to be away from home. Mary thought these friends ungrateful and thought-less — until she met some of the parents. Then she said, "Now I know why some of them feel the way they do. They don't have a family like mine." Still she could not understand the embarrassment of some of her friends from good homes to talk freely of home ties. She was wise enough not to be enticed into the cult of rebellion.

Worse than the friends of family-girl Mary are the cynical teachers and counselors who are suspicious of the desire of any college lad who wants to go home on vaca-tion and of the daughter who confides in her mother. There *are* still healthy home ties. Why make young people feel self-conscious and guilty if they are not rebellious, or do not even need to rebel? Why should a son who had always been free to make choices suddenly be made to feel embarrassed because of a healthy relationship with his father? Why should a daughter who was strong because her mother had given her room to be strong, suddenly be made suspicious of this relationship?

Young men and women are warned against the possessiveness of all parents. Some young people do need this caution, but why disturb those who have healthy family relationships? These we can call manipulated heartaches. There are enough heartaches from broken relationships without creating unnecessary ones. Parents and their growing children need the discernment to know whether their relationships are healthy or not.

It takes experience to grow in discernment. Parents get experience whether they like it or not. But not every parent knows how to learn from his experience.

Every parent remembers the first time his normally dependent, cooperative child rebelled against him and refused his advice. An immature parent will react in defiance and competition with this child who dared to question his authority, but a mature parent will take a good look at this new phenomenon. He will not be blinded by hurt feelings over this seeming rejection of his authority. He will recognize that this is the beginning of the long hard road on which he must learn to discern the difference between the parental protective love needed in childhood and the parental liberating love due an adolescent. Every incident will check the parent on the demands his love has made of his child: whether the demands were out of his own needs or intended to meet the needs of his child.

Maturity and real love are required to face a child's rebellion objectively. It helps greatly to remember that rebellion is a normal part of the growing process. The child is unconsciously crying out that he is a real person in his own right, that he is not the property of his parents, but that he is their responsibility. Within him is the God-implanted yearning to *know who he is*. The child's rebellion may be the unconscious effort to protect his innate yearning to develop his own individuality, which will make him react against domination. This is first of all something fine and strong in him and not something personal against his parents. Whether this rebellion remains healthy or becomes actual rebellion depends upon how the parent reacts to it. The parent who reacts as if his authority were rejected will set his child in a competitive attitude which may lead to dangerous rebellion in adolescence. But the parent who can help his child find himself will know the truth of Tagore's statement: "Let my love like sunlight surround you and give you illumined freedom."

Everything we do for our children from infancy on works toward making them more dependent or more independent. The successful parent works himself out of a job but never out of relationship.

A continued and unbroken relationship depends upon understanding what is really happening to and in a child as he grows out of one experience into another. It always helps to remember that it is *relationship* that must be preserved. One mother missed this important point when she concentrated on her own needs. She was certain that her teen-agers took her for granted as a general servant around the house. One summer she was feeling pinched financially so when one son got a summer job to earn money for college she said to him, "Now you can pay board and room so you will know how much you cost us." The son was horrified: "Don't I belong to this family anymore?" He rebelled against his home being set up as a financial arrangement rather than a relationship. The mother was tired of being taken for granted and she was worried about finances. So she spoke out of her own concerns and not out of her responsibility for a thoughtless son.

A continued and unbroken relationship with a child depends upon what is happening to and in a parent during the process. Is the parent growing from one experience to another? One mother complained, "It seems that no matter what I say to my teen-agers it is the wrong thing. I looked forward to the time when I would have four children in their teens at once, but now I find it a terrifying experience." This mother was as mature as she was beautiful. She began to take stock of herself. She decided she talked too much. To her teen-agers it was "nagging." Disciplining her tongue helped her discipline her irritations. To her surprise her children began to change too. They began to show appreciation for her in many little ways. The crowning experience was the Sunday the youngest and the most rebellious one responded to the pastor's invitation for rededication of life. The mother followed and together they knelt before God. That day began a new relationship which was an inspiration to them all.

These devastating experiences of rebellion and parental shock taken creatively become tests of the quality of parental love. Love can never be taken for granted; it is too easily perverted to self interests.

I like C. S. Lewis' discussion on "need-love" and "gift-love" in *The Four Loves*. He says that need-love is not necessarily selfish because our highest love, our love for God, is need-love.[1] It is after all the only love a baby can have. Every succeeding year in life we all need love. This love is perverted only when it grasps solely for its own benefit when the time for gift-love has come.

We think of gift-love as being like the maternal instinct. As C. S. Lewis points out it is a love that needs to give and therefore needs to be needed.

> But the proper aim of giving is to put the recipient in a state where he no longer needs our gift. We feed children in order that they may soon be able to feed themselves; we teach them in order that they may soon not need our teaching. Thus a heavy task is laid upon this Gift-love. It must work towards its own abdication. We must aim at making ourselves superfluous. The hour when we can say "They need me no longer" should be our reward.[2]

The perversion of gift-love is much more subtle than the perversion of need-love because it is so easy to justify that which gives for another. It will take a higher love to tame

---

[1] New York: Harcourt, Brace & World, 1960, pp. 12-14.
[2] *Ibid.*, p. 76.

"the ravenous need to be needed" which will "gratify itself either by keeping its objects needy or by inventing for them imaginary needs."[3]

Communication seems to be the main difficulty between persons. Somehow or other through the years of close relationship it is so easy to fall into the trap of depending upon words only for communication. A woman said to me the other day, "My husband won't talk to me, he just is no talker." I asked if he communicated any other way. She said she hadn't thought of that.

We should remember from the baby's first months that it takes more than words for communication. At first the baby does not know the words, only the tone of voice and the touch of the hand. When the child first rebels he reacts again to the tone of voice more than to the words themselves. What we are determines the tone of voice. If a mother has anxiety about anything, the anxiety will be communicated to her little ones no matter what words she uses. This is true also as the child grows into adolescence.

Teen years are years of natural frustrations. It is unfortunate when these natural growth frustrations are complicated further by frustrated parents. One mother wrote recently, "How did we ever come to the point where we feel threatened by our young people?" Why are parents frustrated and threatened by their own teen-agers? That is what the parents must find out if they want to be a help and not a hindrance. How do those teen-agers irritate you? That "how" is your point of frustration. Is it because you do not understand them? Or do you feel thwarted by them? If it is in your own feeling then you can do something about it, for your irritation is *your* frustration and *your* responsibility, not theirs. Until that is clarified and conquered, you can do little for your child who is now old enough to do some discerning for himself.

In fact, you are back where you were when they were

---

[3]*Ibid.*, pp. 76-77.

very young. Again, but in a deeper sense, what you are counts more than what you say. Many parents find that now words seem useless, they only antagonize and raise barriers. Of course, the silence of those parents might do the same thing! But this is no time for despair. It is a time for inventory to find out what we really are. Every jolt a rebellious youth gives a parent is a challenge to the parent to look into the mirror to see who he himself is, what he is, and if he is growing. The youth's problem, indeed, is too often merely the reflection of the parent's own problem.

Too often the parent's problem is basically not with his child but with his mate. Over-possessiveness toward the child, domination to the point of meddling, grasping for love response and appreciation are almost certainly from unmet needs and unsolved problems between the child's father and mother. When they were babies, mother alone could give security, but for a teen-ager it takes father *and* mother. Because I believe that an unhappy relationship between father and mother is the greatest cause of a teen-ager's problem most of the chapters in this book will be about husbands and wives. If parents can solve their own problems they will find that many of youth's problems have disappeared into thin air.

Young people cannot be fooled. They always know what the basic parent relationship is. A mother of teen-agers was talking to me not long ago. She said her own parents were very different from each other. Not only were they different, but they differed verbally with each other on many issues, often quite vehemently. She said, "I am surprised that as I remember my teen years I never felt any insecurity because my parents seemed to quarrel. Their disagreements never seemed to do anything to upset their love for one another." Then she added, "Recently we visited Mother and Dad. One day my girls walked in when Mother and Dad were having a hot argument. I was worried about what the girls would think because they loved both grandparents very much. Imagine my surprise that night when one of the girls said, 'I never dreamt that two people as old as Grandma and Granddad could love each other as much as our grandparents love each other!' " The young people saw the unbroken love relationship.

If the days do come when it seems there is little one can do about any problem, there is still a whole field to work in. Dr. Fritz Kunkel called it the "area of free choice." Parents can always work for improvement in the area of their own lives.

Let me suggest that you do not know how much you love your teen-ager until you can be satisfied with the way you love your mate.

So the next question is, how do you love your mate?

2

HOW DO YOU LOVE YOUR MATE?

The greatest word in human relations is *love*. The greatest laboratory for love is in marriage. Much has been done for the preservation of foods but too little for the preservation of love. Young people think they know about love before they really do and too many of the older ones who should know the love that stands the tests of time have become cynical. For this reason many feel like the girl in love for the first time who said, "I can't talk to my mother about love. She wouldn't understand."

Mother and father as husband and wife are under constant observation by their teen-agers who are so curious about adult life. Whether your teen-agers realize it or not they are getting their definitions of love in all its connotations from you, their parents. The most important thing they can learn is to see love as the real essence of your relationship and as a backstop to all the pressures of life. In this they will find security as they enter the threshold of life's insecurities and they will also find a pattern for loving.

But the pathetic and often tragic truth is that many parents do not yet know if or how they love each other. Too often they are like the actress in the process of her fourth divorce who said, "I have no trouble with love. My only problem is with marriage." The oft-quoted statement is true, "It is not marriage that has failed. It is only the people who fail."

We cannot help but wonder why people should fail in a period when there is so much research and literature on the secrets of successful human relations. Even more, why should Christian people fail in the area of love when *God is love* and love is the test of every follower of Christ? (See John 13:35.)

Do we have to admit that parents, with their teen-agers, are too much influenced by the pleasure-ridden mass media of our day? Is the pursuit of personal pleasure of more importance than the fulfillment of personal responsibility. Is the vision so blighted that only the pleasure of the moment is of importance?

No one wants to wait for anything. I see no reason for "instant breakfast" unless time is a factor. (Why lose the taste of bacon and eggs?) But "instants" in food are one thing and "instants" in life are another. You can buy instant coffee but you can't bargain for instant love. You can fool your men folk with instant pudding but love takes a lot of stirring. You may deaden a pain with the pill that does it fastest, but you have to grow into maturity day by day without the benefit of "instant solutions."

The advertisers assure us daily that it is *things* that make the difference in human relations. Things do often make a difference, but they are never the determining factor. If a man's love for his wife is determined by the tinting of her gray hair he is as superficial as the ads. In this day of specializing in human relations it is really strange that the greatest confession of failure in human relations — divorce — is thought of as freedom instead of failure. Even if justified, it is always a confession of failure.

It is misconceptions of life and love that thwart success in living. People quit growing somewhere along the line, so they never really grow up. The surprising fact is that maturity and real love are the same thing. Of course, a three year old is self-centered, he has just reached the age where he has a real consciousness of himself as a person. He must grow on from there into an appreciation of others and his proper relation to them. Of course a sixteen year old is lost in his first feeling of "being in love." He is just getting started and is naturally thrilled with this new exhilarating experience. But anyone who thinks this is all there is to love is headed for disillusionment and probably tragedy. The depths and riches of enduring love are still to be developed. Again the surprising thing is that maturity and real love are the same thing.

So many couples miss the way because they are static in their judgments of their own situations. They judge by "instant satisfaction" without consideration of mature responsibilities. They judge by their own feelings without consideration of others. They blame the other one without seeing their own failures.

An active Sunday school teacher told me he loved his wife but he loved another woman more — a married woman. One day he brought his wife to see me and later he brought the "other woman." These two "fell" into their affair unwittingly while they worked together in the church. Once the "other woman" exclaimed to me, "What can I do? I love him so!" I said, "Do you really? Then do you love him enough to give him up for the sake of your husband, his wife, the church, his future and all the children involved?" That is the test of real love.

One midnight I was awakened by a long-distance telephone call. I was hardly awake yet when I heard a voice sob, "Why doesn't my husband love me in the same way he did at first? How can I know if I love him? What is love anyway?" This wife wanted orchids when she had the deeper joys of love waiting for her in her service to her lovely family.

Someone has said that this decade would go down in

history as one of research into the real meaning of love. Even the secular writers recognize that love is not real mature love until it is giving-love. The New Testament has said this all along. Jesus Himself was the life definition of giving-love.

So we turn first to God and His Word to find out about love. God is love. It is not that God *has* love for us or that He is loving, but that He *is* love. The Old Testament said *God is,* but the New Testament finishes the sentence in Christ to tell us that *God is love.*

Through the Holy Spirit this God-love becomes intrinsic in the Christian. This means that anyone who loves God will also love others because love is genuine in his own life. We read in I John 4:

> Let us go on loving one another, for love comes from God. Every man who truly loves is God's son and has some knowledge of him. But the man who does not love cannot know him at all, for God is love.
> . . . .
> Yes, we love him because he first loved us. If a man says, "I love God" and hates his brother, he is a liar. For if he does not love the brother before his eyes how can he love the one beyond his sight? And in any case it is his explicit command that the one who loves God must love his brother too (verses 7, 8; 19-21, Phillips).

It is seemingly illogical to say that if I do not love my "brother" with all his frailties then I cannot love a perfect God. This bewildered me for years until it dawned on me that God does not love us because we are lovable but because He is love. His every attitude toward us is determined by what He is and not by what we are. The greatest illustration and revelation of this kind of love was in Jesus on the cross. No matter what they did to Him they could get nothing out of Him but love because there was only love in Him.

For everyday living, this means that I can never blame my husband or my neighbor for any reaction I ever have toward them. No matter what happens to me or what anyone does to me, my reactions are always determined by what I am and not by what has been done to me. My own thought and action must begin in my own area of free choice before I begin trying to reform anyone else.

Any woman who gets hold of this truth would find her world revolutionized. The favorite pastime of many wives is the confession of their husband's sins: "My husband doesn't love me anymore, how can I be expected to love him?" "My husband isn't interested in prayer like I am. He leaves me to pray alone."

The men have such "songs" too: "My wife is so absorbed in the children she doesn't know I exist anymore." "When I get home after a hard day I'd like a little peace, but look what I get!"

The daily tendency in life is to think from the self-advantage standpoint. This always leads to self-pity, bitterness, misunderstanding, conflict and ulcers. It takes so little to change this ugly picture — just an about-face in decision and action no matter what the feeling. This is the time to use the disciplines of love even though there is no loving feeling. Love begins all its thought with the need of the other one. The ten lepers who met Jesus were healed as they were on the way in obedience to His direction. In the same way love comes as one is on the way in the action of love.

A young theological student found healing in human relations while on the way. Financial and faculty pressures plus a wife and two active boys in a small Chicago apartment were just too much. "How can anyone have the Holy Spirit in such a situation?" he asked. Then he got a love idea. His first redemptive act toward receiving the Holy Spirit was to buy his wife a box of chocolates, the kind she liked the most — that cost a lot of money! She did not know what was happening so she exclaimed, "Why did you waste the money?" This time he smiled and she knew something had changed. She soon found out that the chocolates were a symbol of new life.

A woman known as a praying woman said one day, "I pray that I may always do the *loving* thing." Her problem was her husband, but her whole image was of herself as a very spiritual person. She wasn't really thinking of her husband and his need, she was thinking of herself being loving in spite of him! When she began to think and pray for her husband's need she found a new love for him. In entering into the exercise of love, giving-love, she found a new sense of partnership in God's love and she also found herself freed from the agony of self-pity.

This is a spiritual law: human and divine relationships are bound together in one package. "Yet if we love one another God does actually live within us, and his love grows in us towards perfection" (I John 4:11, Phillips). If our attention is centered on our own spiritual selves both human and divine relationships are thwarted.

Some years ago at a summer conference Mrs. .... came confessing her husband's sins. She was the "spiritual" one. He was the one responsible for their unhappy years together and for their temporary separation. Through the years she had managed to hold the full sympathy of their two boys, one now married and the other preparing for the ministry. Even though this woman justified her attitudes she still felt guilty, as if she had missed more than happiness. She came to see that her problem was more of an unconscious spiritual arrogance and self-pity than it was of her husband's sins. When she began to think of her husband's side she began to understand why he moved out. So confessing her own sins she asked her husband's forgiveness for the way she had failed him.

Four months later at the noon hour a strange man presented himself at our door with the announcement: "I am Mrs. ....'s husband. She talked to you last summer. We have found a love for one another we never expected possible. She is now critically ill in the hospital. She sent me to you and asked that you talk to me. Please tell me what changed her so much." When I told him about our August conversation, he said, "You know, all these years I blamed her for the failure of our marriage, now I know it was all my fault." (When she quit confessing his sins he was free to confess them himself!) As this man left he said, "If only we had understood more about love when we got married!"

The Scripture that comes closest to the picture of marriage love is one that has often been manhandled by arrogant husbands and feared by defiant wives. It is Paul's discussion of the husband-wife relationship in the fifth chapter of Ephesians. Men have *used* "Wives obey your husbands" as a bolster for waning masculine authority (the masculine mystique), and modern wives of the Western world have hated the Apostle Paul for his "dirty dig" at women. Both are wrong and have entirely missed the secret of a love relationship which Paul presented. This is not a basis for a fight over who dominates whom. The only real authority involved is God's authority. The response of each to the other is "as unto the Lord."

The admonition to husbands and wives follows the general statement of the spiritual law for human relationships: being obedient to or submissive to one another *out of reverence to Christ* (Ephesians 5:21). The love relationship between a Christian husband and wife is not one of competitive domination or submission, but of *function* in loving care. The thoughts of each begin with what is best for the other, a submission to the best welfare of the other *out of reverence for Christ.*

Such love eliminates all fear (I John 4:18). The husband is to love his wife as Christ loved the Church and that is enough love for any woman! Such love is manifested in sacrificial love and care. Such sacrifice or service (servanthood) is synonymous with the authority vested in God-love (giving-love) and is never a threat to the authority of the headship of man to woman, or to the dignity of personal fulfillment of woman.

When Paul stated the general spiritual law of concern for another he applied it first to the function of wifehood. I cannot believe this was discrimination against women; rather it was a conviction that the women, who are created to be mothers, would understand first what he meant by this kind of giving-love. In spite of all the equality demanded by women's rights advocates, the fact still remains that only women can bear the babies. And the wise Creator would surely give woman special capacity for love and care in such a human responsibility. This is not to her credit or discredit but defines her unique ministry in human relations. The woman who knows this wonderful gift will minister to the needs of each member of her family without fear of being "walked over" or of being depersonalized.

The other day I read about a Little League baseball player who came to sit in line with the expectant fathers in a hospital corridor. The distraught, waiting men wondered what he wanted. He told them a big game was in progress and he was sitting in for the expectant umpire. But no one could sit in for the umpire's wife!

When husband and wife are both set free because of the individual commitment of each to the God who is love they have the best chance in the world to find real union with each other without blotting out the personality of either one. The whole story of the marriage relationship in Ephesians five is introduced by *walk in love* (v. 2) and *be filled with the Spirit* (v. 18).

But what about the marriage in which only one partner has accepted the love of God as a working force in life? Even here there is no alibi for self-pity or escape from a difficult position. Love does not withdraw in self-defense but reaches out to the need of the other one.

> In the same spirit you married women should adapt yourselves to your husbands, so that even if they do not obey the Word of God they may be won to God without any word being spoken, simply by seeing the pure and reverent behavior of you, their wives. Your beauty should not be dependent on an elaborate coiffure, or on the wearing of jewelry or fine clothes, but on the inner personality — the unfading loveliness of a calm and gentle spirit, a thing very precious in the eyes of God (I Peter 3:1-4, Phillips).

It is so easy to fall into the misconception that communication is by words only. A woman with a non-Christian husband is to witness by what she is rather than by her words. That means she must *be* Christian, she must truly represent the love of God as revealed in Christ by the way she lives everyday. If she learns this she is not only a good wife but a good mother.

Teen-agers can pick at and resent words, but they have a hard time fighting the dignity of good living. The so-called American neurosis — pressure to compete, to succeed, to achieve, to win — makes parents push their children. The anxiety of pushing always leads to many words. The quietness of inner strength is irresistible and much more effective.

If you have found yourself and know yourself as a person, you will be much better equipped to help your children know themselves as persons.

If you know the disciplines of love in your own life, you will be much better able to direct the growing self-disciplining in your teen-agers.

If you have achieved mature love which goes far beyond romantic love but still appreciates romance for what it is, you will be giving your teen-ager discernments by which he can judge his own experiences.

If you love your mate in spite of differences and difficulties, your security in your relationship to one another will help your adolescent find the security he so desperately seeks.

If you have learned to love your mate in a mature way, you will easily avoid the pitfalls of possessiveness and domination (bossiness) which are so detrimental to your children.

If your teen-agers have jogged you awake to any failure in yourself or in your relationship to one another, you can show them how to grow on correction. The touchstone for all this testing is love, giving-love.

This love of which I speak is slow to lose patience — it looks for a way of being constructive.
It is not possessive:
it is neither anxious to impress
nor does it cherish inflated ideas of its own importance.
  Love has good manners
and does not pursue selfish advantage.
It is not touchy.

It does not keep account* of evil
or gloat over the wickedness of other people.
On the contrary, it is glad with all good men when truth
prevails.
Love knows no limit to its endurance,
no end to its trust,
no fading of its hope;
it can outlast anything.
It is, in fact, the one thing that still stands when all else
has fallen.

(I Corinthians 13:4-7, *Phillips*)

3

HOW DO YOU LOVE GOD?

A reappraisal of one's love in marriage will automatically bring into focus a reappraisal of one's relationship to God. It is just as easy to take God for granted as it is to take one's mate for granted. Taking a mate or God for granted leads to boredom when every day should be bringing exciting new discoveries of relationship. We take God for granted when we make lesser things more important.

We can fall into unspiritual habits by finding a temporary security in the *forms* of our worship while forgetting the love of the God we worship. We can depend upon our confidence in the accepted *orthodoxy* of our faith and fall into the greatest heresy of all — lack of love. (See John 13:35.) "By this shall all men know that ye are my disciples, that ye love one another." We may be absorbed in the *activities* of our service in the church so that we think we are justified by our works. We may even short-change our children of loving care because

---

*Compile statistics in the first edition of *Letters to Young Churches*.

of our religious busyness. Whenever fervor for the Lord becomes a fever in activity we have lost our way.

Sometime ago I was brought up with a start by the verse, "Every man who truly loves is God's son and has some knowledge of him. But the man who does not love cannot know him at all, for God is love." (I John 4:7, 8, *Phillips*) Sounds unorthodox, doesn't it? But the greatest heresy is always failure to love. A fever in doing "God's work" is a failure in love. It is being lost in things instead of being found in a growing relationship.

The fever of anxiety about *things* and *prestige* is the subtle way parents may be caught thwarting the warmth of love in their home relationships also. One mother told me that the most hectic hour of the week in their household was the last hour on Sunday morning before they left for Sunday school. From the time they got up it was "Hurry! Hurry! Hurry! We mustn't be late!" Breakfast was hectic, the little ones wanted to know what to wear, and the teen-agers wanted to know where their clothes got to! By the time everyone was ready and they were all on the way to Church no one felt like worshiping. The little ones pinched each other, the teen-agers picked on Mother, and Mother tore into Dad.

I can hear Jesus speak to such parents: "You are anxious and troubled about many things. Organize your *things* on Saturday so relationships can be more important as you prepare to worship on Sunday."

Inner frustration and the compulsion to push other people around are always evidences of being out of the center of God's peace and love. Pushing other people around is usually followed by blaming others for one's own spiritual failure. This is a sure sign that the inner citadel is empty. In such hours Walter Rauschenbusch's words have always drawn me back to center:

> In the castle of my soul
> Is a little postern gate,
> Whereat, when I enter,
> I am in the presence of God.
> In a moment, in the turning of a thought,

I am where God is.
This is a fact.

When I enter into God,
All life has meaning.
Without asking I know;
My desires are even now fulfilled,
My fever is gone
In the great quiet of God . . .[1]

When inner fever is reduced in this great reverent quiet of God, a sense of renewed faith blots out the frustrating anxieties that seemed so important before. With the grace of renewal comes a consciousness of authority in God's love which deletes all possessiveness and bossiness. This brings the marvelous discovery that in the moment of greatest need one may find the Source of power that seemed so elusive in the midst of all that agonizing self-effort.

There is an answer in Christ for all those times when the heart cries out helplessly, "I do not have the power." For some strange reason people take it for granted that they can get extra power for "spiritual" work, but fail to realize that the same adequate power is available for everyday living. What witness does a church-going woman have to her non-Christian neighbor if she succumbs to the same irritations and despairs with her husband and children as her neighbor does? In fact the church woman is worse off, because she feels guilty when she fails and so she becomes even more frustrated.

An active church woman said, "I love my church work, I love my quiet days at home, but the evening I cannot take. My husband lets down from his hard day, the children burst out at the seams in every way. I don't feel spiritual at all when I am with my family. I'd like to run away." But this husband had a hard time, too. He did have a hard day. He looked forward to the comforts of home. But what did he find? A wife sorry for herself, perhaps too tired from church activities even to get a good

---

[1]From *Walter Rauschenbusch* by Dores Robinson Sharpe (New York: The Macmillan Company, 1942). Italics mine.

meal for her family! And the children? Life at school was hectic and they feel frustrated. Then when they get home both parents are frustrated! What a mess. *Words* about the Church or about the Christian life won't mean much to those children.

But there is good news for despairing parents caught in the pitfalls of ragged nerves. A grandfather recently found this out. He always dreaded visiting his children because the grandchildren got on his nerves. (He stayed out of the way as much as possible when his own were small.) But after coming into a new experience of Christ he was greatly surprised when he visited his daughter to find out that he also had a new love for children. He was not even expecting this. And strange to say "the children were different." The new Granddaddy made new children!

Discovering the secret of love by grace releases one from being a prisoner of his own feelings. When we find it so hard to love other people or to be patient in difficult situations it is encouraging to know that God has provided a power to help us out. "How tremendous is the power available to us who believe in God. That power is the same divine energy which was demonstrated in Christ when he raised him from the dead" (Ephesians 1:19, 20, *Phillips*). It is beyond our human comprehension to realize that this power is the same power by which Jesus was resurrected! But we can experience this power by faith.

The Apostle Paul said this new disposition is a *fruit* of the Spirit:

> The Spirit, however, produces in human life fruits such as these: love, joy, peace, patience, kindness, generosity, fidelity, tolerance, and self-control — and no law exists against any of them.
>
> Those who belong to Christ Jesus have crucified their old nature with all that it loved and lusted for. If our lives are centered in the Spirit, let us be guided by the Spirit (Galatians 5:22-25, Phillips).

Part of the difficulty in taking God for granted is that we have not taken His promises seriously. And even when we try to be different we try in our own strength and, of course, become discouraged. Perhaps we need to go back to the beginning of our Christian lives. Some churches have marriage anniversary services. When husbands and wives of all ages stand there hand in hand and renew their original vows something is bound to happen. Some are embarrassed at expressing undying love to one another. (Perhaps they have just finished a quarrel!) Some are shy at their voiced words of devotion because they have lost the art of love communication. But the faces of some glow with the realization of the depths of love they have found since they first took those vows.

Going back to the beginning of our relationship to God we may ask ourselves about the authenticity of the new relationship. Almost always it was real in the beginning but we forgot about the needed growth in relationship. It is never too late to renew those original vows in marriage or with God. A new start can always profit by past mistakes. But it must be remembered that the new disposition is a *fruit* of the Holy Spirit. Our commitment was and is to Christ, who is our living Lord. He "disappeared" from this earth, but He is not an absent Lord. The Holy Spirit is the true agent of His Presence. (Read John 16:7.)

One of the hardest lessons to learn as we grow in the Lord and in human relationships is how much to depend upon how we feel. In fact the question is, whether we can ever depend upon how we feel. We feel below par sometimes because we are too tired. Then a rest is called for and not self-accusation. The only point of concern is — are one's commitment to God and relationship to others in good condition?

The danger for a new Christian or a new bride is that the glow of love may be in time treasured for the glow and not the love. Having once had a "holy feeling" doesn't automatically make one holy. Having no holy feeling does not say that you are not wholly God's. It is maintaining and growing in the relationship that counts. The fact is that a husband and wife may be closer to each other when they are going through some hard experience *togethe*r with no energy left for ecstacy than in their greatest moments of rapture. The same is true in our relationship to God (our "spiritual" condition). As we follow through the disciplines of love in daily life, in the midst of unlovely people and difficult circumstances there will be little emotion left for us to feel holy. But God knows — and children discern — that love *lived* is more dynamic and real than love that is only felt.

We must know the meaning of love that is beyond feeling to have courage for everyday living. Our relationship to God need never be changed by any circumstances, no matter how we feel. This is also true in human relationships. Circumstances are not the controlling factor in good relationships. In fact untoward circumstances should make any good relationship much stronger.

Often times God uses the things that happen to us to bring us closer to Him. Some of us have to get shocked awake. That's my story.

We were in the mountains in India for our first vacation in our second term of missionary service. I was having disposition problems which my good husband excused for health reasons, but deep in my heart I knew better. Three warnings hit me in one week. On Tuesday I scolded my daughter, Lois, according to my irritation and not according to her deed. With eight-year-old candor she looked up at me and said, "Mother, why can't you be kind to me like Mrs. B. is to her little girl?" On Friday of that week I got impatient with my husband because I thought he was delaying too long in getting something done. He looked at me in his quiet way and said, "What would the churches in America think if they saw you now?" On Sunday morning in Sunday School class the Bible teacher made the statement, "We are before God the size we are before our families."

That was the end of me! I had to face the fact that I did not lose my temper before the Indians or the other missionaries, only with my family. My spiritual pride was stronger than my love for my family. I knew now that I desperately needed the kind of spiritual life and love that would benefit my loved ones. I looked to the Heavenly

Father as I had never done before. He showed me the secret of His grace. That was thirty-three years ago. I haven't graduated yet, but thank God, I am still learning! And I know now where to turn in any hour of need.

Paul didn't tell the Corinthian Christians that the Holy Spirit is given merely to make one feel good. He said the Spirit is given for the *common good* (I Corinthians 12:7). *For the common good* will bring blessing to our families first of all. When our children see that we are able to meet pressures, conflicts, frustrations, disappointments, failures and reproofs they will see the way through such experiences for themselves. They can argue against our much talking but never against God's life lived out before them.

Even though every person's experience of God is his own individual experience, still not one of us can come to Him exclusive of others. Therefore *we* come. It is "*Our* Father — give *us our* daily bread, forgive *us* as *we* forgive others." This is especially true of persons so closely involved as a married couple. Neither one can have a full experience of God without involving the other one, either in fellowship in the Lord or in the redemptive love of the Lord. If this were fully realized it would put an end to the "spiritual one" feeling bereft because he is alone in his relationship to God. The one who knows God has no room for self-pity if he takes his Christian responsibility toward the unbelieving mate. In fact the unbelieving mate is consecrated through his believing mate (I Corinthians 7:14).

The spiritual relationship in marriage, whether mutual or not, is by way of God. Just one person loving God can make it a holy triangle; husband, wife and God. Marriage is not just two persons, it is two persons and God. If *both* look beyond themselves to God they will find a union together which is never possible if they think only of one another.

Many consider this as a general law for successful marriage even if God is not considered. Antoine de Saint-Exupery, a French author writing in the first half of this century said it wisely, "Love does not consist in gazing at each other but in looking outward together in the same direction." Recent research concludes the same thing: "In marriage, lovers look not at the 'self' as in childhood nor at each other as during courtship and the honeymoon, but in the same direction, for their union does not exist alongside of life, it is a way of life."[2] When the two look out together to God, the chances for the greatest fulfillment in life are almost certain.

Men who have gone through hardships in life without losing any youthful idealism are the ones who give us courage today. Such a man was Eberhard Arnold, a YMCA secretary in Germany during the First World War. He entered into the idealism of the German Youth movement after the war and out of this experience he founded the Society of Brothers. This fellowship has been tested in their commitment to the love of God in family and community in experiences on three continents. Eberhard Arnold wrote about *love divine and human*:

> One who enters into the eternal oneness of two before God, experiences the blessing of this sacred mystery in his own body and spirit. God has compared His covenant with His people and the unity of Christ and His Church to this union of betrothal and marriage. The one eternal Christ is the single object of devotion of His Church; He kindles in her all the powers of love and of the Spirit. In the same way, complete unity is given in marriage, a unity which awakens and unfolds all the powers of manhood and motherly womanhood. Marriage, which is the will of two to create something beyond themselves, is a participation in God's creative power. In our spiritual life this participation should awaken all our energies for God's essence, His will, and His love to all. . . . Thus our love life becomes our destiny in the most serious sense of the word. . . .
>
> The warmth that comes from God's heart cannot be produced in any laboratory, by any decree, or by any organization. No friendly efforts or zealous benevolence can imitate this genuine gold. . . . Love begets love. . . . Hence the love that is Agape . . . bears the character of Him who literally pours it out over us. . . .
>
> Agape seeks and demands nothing for itself because it lives completely in the object of its love. It knows nothing of rights,

---

[2]*Marriage: A Psychological and Moral Approach*, Wm. C. Bier, S.J., ed. (New York: Fordham University Press, 1965), p. 128.

for its nature is to abandon and forget the standpoint of rights, to find its happiness in giving.[3]

Many of the problems in the Corinthian Church came because they had forgotten the real meaning of love. They were very religious, it is true, but they made their own religious experience an end in itself, they quarreled with one another over church leadership, their own religious merits and they had many marriage problems. Still they were very religious. This is the reason Paul wrote to them:

> If I were to speak with the combined eloquence of men and of angels I should stir men like a fanfare of trumpets or the crashing of cymbals, but unless I had love, I should do nothing more.
>
> If I had the gift of foretelling the future and had in my mind not only all human knowledge but the secrets of God, and if, in addition, I had that absolute faith which can move mountains, but had no love, I tell you I should amount to nothing at all.
>
> If I were to sell all my possessions to feed the hungry and, for my convictions, allowed my body to be burned, and yet had no love, I should achieve precisely nothing.

(I Corinthians 13:1-3, Phillips)[4]

In everyday words Paul is saying that to be spiritual means to be loving in everyday life. We cannot be truly spiritual in public life unless we live this kind of love in our private lives.

Teen-agers grow into their definitions of love of God and love of one another by what they know of their parents' relationship to one another and to God. It isn't the number of prayers parents pray but what difference praying makes that speaks to youth. They must see power for living to know that such power is available.

Are you concerned about your teen-agers' faith? He can't really imitate you, he will have to make your faith, if authentic, his own. In the process of making it his own he will have many honest doubts, but you need not have

---

[3]*Love and Marriage in the Spirit,* (Rifton, N. Y.: Plough Publishing House, 1965), p. 10.

[4]*Letters to Young Churches,* 1947 edition. Copyright 1947, The Macmillan Company.

undue concern. If you have *lived* your faith he will never be able to forget it.

If you have truly loved God you have set your family free to love Him and you have shown your children that only in such love is there fulfillment of life.

4

HOW DO YOU LOVE YOURSELF?

> For whoever wishes to save his life will lose it, and whoever, for my sake, loses his life shall find it. (Matthew 16:25, *Twentieth Century*)[1]
>
> I have come that they may have Life and may have it in greater fulness. (John 10:10, *Twentieth Century*)

These two statements of Jesus seem paradox enough, but add to them *Love thy neighbor as thyself*, and one can easily become bewildered. The question is, are we in a real dilemma or on the verge of a great new secret? How can I lose myself and still find my own fulfillment? How can I lose myself and still love myself and find in that love of myself a gauge for my love for others?

The problem is *how* to love one's self, or one's life. Jesus was talking more about *finding* life than losing it, but something must be given up before life can be found. Perhaps the cue is in the phrase, "wishes to save his life." This is the self-centered approach. This is the only approach a small child has because he is just discovering himself and his relation to others in his environment. But an adult who is self-centered is truly "lost." He is not free because he is driven by forces and emotions he

---

[1]Chicago: Moody Press.

does not understand. He is dependent upon acceptance of others at the same time that he is rebelling against them. He does not know himself because he is torn by inner conflicts. His reactions to others are out of these inner conflicts rather than a clear objective reaction to the other person. His growth is stunted. He feels bound — and he is bound.

Dr. Karen Horney helps us to see that it is a false self we give up so that the *real self* can have a chance at life. "The real self is the alive, unique, personal center of ourselves; the only part that can, and wants to grow."[2] So he who wishes to save his false, immature self will lose his life, and whoever, for Christ's sake, loses his false self will find life in his real self. This would be a paradox indeed if the purpose were only for self-realization. That motivation would be dangerously near self-centeredness. So the secret is in giving one's self to Christ who wants only fullness of life for everyone of His followers.

This losing one's self for Christ's sake is what is often called "being saved." But many people miss the fullness of the abundant life because they do not realize that salvation is not a static experience. It is a *living* experience. Being born into the family of God is only the beginning of new life. The real self is now set free for growth into the fullness of the stature of Christ (See Ephesians 4:13.) The forgiving grace of God takes away all debilitating guilt; the loving grace of God brings the living, enabling power of God for growth in this grace. Life is no longer an "obstacle race" but a race in which every obstacle is a means of growth.

As one learns about God's love the desire to lose one's life in Him grows. The place to begin a new life is with God because with Him there is the least fear of obliteration of one's self. Such a commitment of life always brings the surprise of newness of life. What was "lost" no

---

[2]*Neurosis and Human Growth* (New York: W. W. Norton & Co., 1950), p. 155.

longer counts. A young college girl wrote her mother after she had dedicated her life to God and His service, "I feel like a whole person for the first time in my life!"

A new sense of dignity that gives an unexpected self-respect is another surprise after losing one's old self to God. After the Samaritan woman had been treated as a real person by Christ she won the respect of her neighbors who must have despised her before. A business man who in his private life alternated between self-depreciation and lording it over his wife now has no compulsion to do either, for he has found dignity and self-respect in a new experience in Christ.

This dignity which gives self-respect helps one to see himself as God values him; therefore because he knows God loves him, he can love himself. The very fact that each one of us is so important to God never makes one cocky; rather, it brings the humility that is born of God-consciousness and is never colored with self-depreciation.

As one grows in this consciousness of being loved by God one becomes aware that God loves other people in the same way. This means that they will be considered by us as God sees them. (See II Corinthians 5:16) The discipline of seeing others as God sees them is a revolutionary experience: the people who irritate me, the ones who do not like me, the ones who seem to make my way hard — God loves them all and wants them redeemed!

In the kingdom of God, love is the ruling force, but the secular world around us brings the pressure of a different kind of thinking. The secular world begins with self-interest in personal, professional and national affairs. Power is the goal and this power uses *fear* as a tool. In the kingdom of God power is also a big word, but God's power uses *love* as a tool. (See II Timothy 1:7) The Christian has to find out how to relate to this world around him. What does he do in his relationship to others, to those who have power over him and to those over whom he has power?

We are interested especially in the way this struggle has affected the relationship of men and women, husbands and wives. This struggle may have been going on since the day that Adam blamed Eve for his sin, but the struggle has been out in the open in the Western world ever since the Feminist movement began in England with the publication of Mary Wollstonecraft's *A Vindication of the Rights of Women* in 1792. She insisted that women should have every "right" that men have. The end of that struggle came with *Modern Woman: The Lost Sex* published by Harper's in 1947. Woman couldn't be man, so she might just as well try to find her fulfillment as a woman!

In the meantime the tide had already been reversed. Following two world wars Western culture turned to an appreciation of the *feminine* rather than the feminist qualities. Woman's sphere was again accepted as being first of all in the home as wife and mother. Women seemed to accept this renewed emphasis on a woman's femininity with gladness, even though they listed their occupation as "just a housewife."

The rush for the "feminine role" has become so great that early marriage statistics have become shocking and tragic. Even brilliant women have been afraid to finish their education for fear marriage would pass them by.

There were other changes which affected the family. Suburbia developed. Modern gadgets and labor-saving devices took the drudgery and some creativity out of housework. Talented women had time on their hands and became restless. The social life of children became so accelerated that they were thrust into experiences beyond their years and mother had to become the family chauffeur. Then mother began to feel victimized as if the whole family used her. Self-pity made her wonder about her own rights.

Something was happening to the man of the house too. He was becoming known as the "vanishing American father." He was never around when mother had problems with the children. When he was home he wanted rest and not another set of responsibilities. However, the "masculine mystique" has not changed. Although father has abdicated his responsibility of headship in the home

41

he still is not ready to give up his masculine prestige. He feels victimized, too, by being ignored and he usually compensates by lording it over his wife for her failures in carrying the double load. He lords it over the children when they get in the way of his "home comforts." It is hard for anyone to find the real authority so essential to family security as well as to individual freedom.

The frustrated women of America (too many of them church women) responded en masse to Betty Friedan's *The Feminine Mystique* in 1963 (Norton). They heard her speak for them as she found the "problem that has no name." The whole controversy was brought further into focus by the Commission on the Status of Women appointed by President Kennedy. But Margaret Mead, the anthropologist, said that in spite of the good work of this commission the essential questions remained unanswered. (*Redbook*, November 1963).

Dozens of magazines, both secular and religious have featured critiques of the "feminine mystique," ranging from special appeals for motherhood as a full-time job to appeals for careers plus family responsibilities. In spite of all the discussions the basic issue still remains: how does one find individual identity and personal fulfillment while giving one's life in service to others? Women — and men — are still afraid that in serving others they are losing out in their own fulfillment of life.

I have often wondered if the women of India are not much closer to the secret of this fulfillment than Western women, even Christian Western women. In a Bombay home in 1964 a group of us fell to discussing modern women. Those present were from the United States, New Zealand and India. On the coffee table before us was a Canadian national magazine which started the discussion. Its critique of *The Feminine Mystique* implied that women in this second revolt of modern women were after what the suffragettes failed to get: the right of every woman to "fulfill herself." The Indian woman in our group seemed the least concerned by the modern woman's fears. She could remember when she had no "rights," but she seemed to have a smile which originated from some place of inner quiet from which she made her observations. I think she knew that even when she had no "rights" she had something so much deeper, something within her which could not be enslaved or penned up. Her "rights" in new India (more than in America!) were appreciated, but still peripheral to her basic security and fulfillment. We American women can well ask, "What does she have that I don't have?"

In spite of seeming self-negation through the centuries, Indian women have been strong, not weak. The very backbone of the Freedom Movement led by Mahatma Gandhi was the strength of India's women. They did not mind hardships. They could lose themselves in the Cause without fear or self-pity, and they have entered into the fresh liberties granted them in New India without any tendency to license. They are still the most womanly of the world's women.

When my husband and I first went to India in the twenties I expected to find Indian women, especially the village women, namby-pamby, submissive and weak. One of the greatest surprises of my life was their enormous inner strength. Seeming negation never hurt Indian women.

In our land where the fundamental principle of democracy is the inherent worth of every individual, too many people think of "self-surrender" as a complete loss of identity. They even think that a philosophy of fulfillment through service to others is a negation of self. One lecturer said no sane person could accept such an idea.

I agree that no sane person negates himself. But negation has never been a Christ concept. No one ever placed more value on each individual, irrespective of sex or social position, than Jesus did. In fact, He shocked the "good" people of His day by showing human respect for the most disreputable sinners, including women! How can anyone with intelligence infer that Jesus would show less respect for individual worth than modern democracy might? But for Jesus what we think of as democracy and fulfillment of life in service to others were one and the same thing. As a Christian concept they are not opposites. The inherent worth of one individual includes the fact of the inherent worth of *every* individual. This is where God-love which is giving-love makes the transfer from childhood's receiving-love to maturity's giving-love. This is not the pious admonition of a clergyman but a statement of the law of life for the finding of one's own identity and one's personal fulfillment.

Jesus said it because it is true: "For whoever would save his life will lose it, and whoever loses his life for my sake will find it" (Matthew 16:25), and "The Son of Man came not to be ministered unto, but to minister, and to give his life a ransom for many" (Matthew 20: 28, KJ). This is the paradox for fulfillment of life abundant. It is the secret in the Beatitudes and in the Cross. It was true for Jesus. It is true for His followers. No one ever finds fulfillment in the process of protecting his own rights any more than one finds love by looking for it. Fulfillment comes as one matures out of self-centeredness into love, and love comes by giving love. This is never understood until it is lived because it sounds so paradoxical.

The basic admonition that the apostle gave for all Christians was to "walk in love" (Ephesians 5:2) as Christ did. His general principle for walking in love in personal relationships is "Be subject to one another out of reverence for Christ" (Ephesians 5:21). This means that the fundamental principle of every one in Christ in relation to others is that of giving consideration *first* to the best welfare of the *other* person. One's first thought may never be for the protection of his own prestige, authority or selfish interest. When self-centered interests come first they are not in reverence for Christ; therefore they are not Christian.

This spiritual law of love in concern for another shows up clearly in the marriage relationship because marriage is the closest human relationship possible. Paul's strongest love admonition is to the husband who carries the responsibility of headship to his wife and in his family: "Husbands, love your wives, as Christ loved the church and gave himself up for her" (Ephesians 5:2). What wife wouldn't submit herself to a love like that!

The definition for the husband's headship is Christ's headship of the Church: "The Son of Man came not to be ministered unto but to minister . . ." And I, a woman, would say most heartily that any normal woman would give deep reverence to such headship. Such love always begets love.

The authority vested in the headship of Christ was not something apart from His servanthood, but an intrinsic part of it. This is hard for us in our world to understand. It is beyond our comprehension until we, by faith, act upon giving-love. The ability to live this kind of love everyday is created in us through the power of the Holy Spirit.

When we separate authority from servanthood then authority becomes domineering. A man *demands* recognition of headship when he has forfeited its responsibility and a woman who is not in Christ becomes rebellious and disdainful. These attitudes are even worse among the very "religious" who are still self-centered for they use God's words as an argument for their selfish demands. Jesus had a parable for those who were arrogant and who despised others even as they prayed. (See Luke 18:9-14.)

And the wife! Woman is created with the capacity to have a love that can lose itself for others. How else can she be a real mother? A woman who cannot give herself for others is a frustrated woman, an unfulfilled woman. Listen to a man speak:

> Woman is born to be LOVE — in every form of expression. It is her life-long work, her true feminine function. It is the miracle-working power of God, and she is privileged indeed to be given this high duty.
>
> She can only achieve this wondrous state of fulfillment when the full gospel of Jesus Christ is set up in her heart. . . . Here is the central secret of her being, and the only way to fulfill herself.
>
> * * *
>
> The law of love is irrevocable and infallible in its working. . . . That is why, in every situation, a woman should be

> identified with the Father's all-embracing plan. She *must* recognize her spiritual potential and her oneness with the Lord. . . . Otherwise she is bound to the grinding wheel of cause and effect . . . and becomes a slave. . . .[3]

When a woman gives herself in devotion to her family this does not preclude activities outside the home. She will not, however, be seeking fulfillment elsewhere *in spite of* her family but as an integral part of her family relationship.

If you have learned to love yourself because God loves you, if you love your mate for himself as God loves him, then you have lost your fear of losing your own identity for you are finding the fulfillment that comes from God-love.

Your teen-agers are trying to find out who they are and what life is all about. If you, their parents, have found personal dignity and freedom, full security in the love of God and fulfillment in the joy of living, your children will not rebel against walking in your footsteps. By your life you will set your teen-ager free to find his own individual life fulfillment under the drawing power of the love of God.

[3]Brother Mandus, *For Women Only* (Evesham, Worcs., England: Arthur James, Ltd.), pp. 27, 30.

Part Two
LOVE LIVED

5

LOVE'S DISCIPLINE ENLIVENS MONOTONY

"In this life we have three great lasting qualities —
faith, hope and love. But the greatest of them is love"
(I Corinthians 13:13, Phillips).

"Love is a many-splendored thing." That is what your
teen-agers hear. They hear about thrills, ecstasies, excitement. When they think they have found love, they decide
that it is even more wonderful than all they have heard.
If they think this is all there is to love, where have you,
their parents, been?

This chapter is for parents who are bogged down in
their love journey. Did you think that marriage was the
end of the story like the love stories you read in your teens?
Or have you found that love is the most enduring quality
in the world?

Or — are you disillusioned with love? Have you lost its
sister qualities, faith and hope? As you have learned to
know your mate have you taken it for granted that he or
she cannot change or grow? Have you lost faith in your
mate's possibilities for improvement and therefore lost
hope for your future? Still you are mature enough not to
seek a way of escape. You take each other for granted,
you circumvent possible clashes of temperament, you endure your incompatibilities for any of twenty reasons. You
have set yourself for a long endurance race. How
monotonous!

They used to call marriage *settling down*. The problem

is *how* to settle down. Have you merely settled down by resigning yourself to an endurance test? This may turn out to be a monotony that is synonymous with monogamy — as some facetiously describe it. But the problem is not in the monogamy. Polygamy would not solve anything.

To your teen-aged children your marriage may look like the dictionary's synonyms for monotony: "dull, tedious, wearisome, wearying, unvaried, undiversified, tiresome, irksome, uninteresting, humdrum, prosy, slow, dry, drowsy, heavy, depressive, flat!" If any of these words speak to your condition, you'd better lift up your eyes and hope for new life, for anyone can change if love is accepted *with* its disciplines.

If you are disillusioned for lack of excitement, the kind your teen-agers seem to need, there is a greater excitement awaiting you on the mature level. This is the satisfying excitement that comes from finding the secret of life in the midst of seeming deadness. It is also the satisfying joy of having part in the creation of a new situation out of a bad one. It is above all the satisfaction of entering a new relationship with the one who had brought you life's highest hopes and now seems to have given you only disappointment.

If you have accepted failure as your lot in life and have given up any hope for real fulfillment of personal joy in your marriage you have not settled down as our grandparents meant it. You have merely short-changed your mate by going dead on his hands. Grandmother meant it was time to quit looking everywhere for entertainment and to settle down to the responsibilities of life.

You may think you have done this when you bring in the support for the family or when you faithfully do the housekeeping. Being faithful in the mechanics of living is important, but actually it is only a superficial part of marriage. The real *settling down* is not to the monotony of a work-a-day world but to the dynamics of an ever renewing relationship. You may have thought at the beginning that your marriage was made in heaven, but you must admit it was bungled on earth. And on earth, with God's help you can have every wasted day and year redeemed — through the discipline of love.

Too many Western moderns are afraid of discipline, even of divine discipline. Even people who believe in the free grace of God want God to hand it out to them without their assuming any of the responsibility of acceptance. God did not make us that way. He does not want human puppets. He made us to be responsible persons. He waits for us to learn to come to Him and to choose His ways.

Our first discipline is the *acceptance of love*. We have seen that God's love includes not only me but all others, including my "better half." Sometimes we accept this new way of life like the mountain boy who had the reputation of being the best fighter in the community. The day after he was baptized one of the boys who was always afraid to tackle him now began to taunt him for not fighting. This new Christian didn't want to fight — he had given that up — but he wasn't quite ready to take taunts for being yellow. He turned to the next best fighter and said, "You fight him for me. I can't fight, I was just baptized!"

Too many put all the responsibility for the "good fight" onto God without taking their own responsibility in their affairs. Some people even go so far as to rejoice when suffering comes to those who have hurt them, as if God were fighting for them. The pesky thing is that God loves the other person as much as He does us!

Obedience to the discipline of love has no relation to any forced obedience that may have given one a reaction against obedience. This obedience is more the quality of the discipline of the musician and the athlete. One of my sons took me to a World Series baseball game some years ago for a birthday present. Both teams were so good that day that no one could score a run. It looked so easy. In fact, to me, it looked like they were mechanical beings out there in the field. Years of discipline lay back of that game. The players had practiced strenuously, but without strain, until they could play in faith without anxiety.

When you accept the discipline of God-love it will

reverse the first big mistake you made which led your marriage into this stalemate. You thought you knew your mate when you went to the altar together, but in the intimacy of life together you found out many things you did not know before your marriage began. Then you felt disillusioned and disappointed and finally you gave up to an acceptance of failure and unhappiness. All this time you have been thinking about the faults of the other one which you decided you would have to endure for the rest of your life. Disillusionment led to accusation and accusation to defense and defense to lonely despair.

The way back is not to begin with your mate's faults, but with your own. Surely you haven't been perfect either. So the first step in accepting the way of love is to face one's own failure in the marriage.

When you decide to look at your own failures you'd better begin with God and His forgiving love or you will hate yourself for what you have been. So begin with His love for you, then look at yourself honestly. Perhaps by now you could be objective enough to list all the things about which your mate has accused you. Many of his accusations may be more subjective than objective; i.e. they may come out of his own conflicts rather than from the failure he sees in you, but they will provide food for thought anyway. Look at them honestly and bravely. Some of them will show you clearly where you have failed your mate.

Now you come to the real question; do you want to change? If so, you will gain time in growth by working on what your life partner has unwittingly suggested. You can be thankful for his insight (or hers) and confess your own sins, not your mate's. You will be surprised at the results of your change of action. Somehow the air will be cleared and monotony will be blown out the window.

Not only will monotony be gone but new life is contagious. The first thing you know your mate will also enter into the excitement of mature growth. This takes longer with some people than with others, but it always works with reasonable people, and these things take place:

Your faith is in God.

Your faith is in His way of love.

You maintain your own commitment to God.

You confess your own sins and let your mate care for his.

You accept correction from your mate and others without having your feelings hurt.

You quit pushing others around.

You turn to your mate to understand him (or her) better.

Adolescent years are exciting years — even frustrations are dramatic. Imagine what is happening when this growth excitement is wet-blanketed by parents living in deadening monotony! If you have found your way out of the morass of monotony, you will show your children the excitement of living which is deeper than anything they dreamed possible. You will show them an exciting courage that brings hope in any hour of despair.

If you are church people, it is all the more important to escape the deadness that comes to some relationships. You have not only your relationship as parents and its effect on your adolescents to nurture but you also carry the responsibility of helping them to know how God-love works out in everyday living. You want them to know God, to know how to make creative use of His love. They must learn that first from you.

God's love is the most dramatic, the most exciting fact of life. Living in His love disintegrates monotony. Let your children learn from your lives together that there are lasting interesting qualities in the Christian life, that active participation in faith, hope and love need not, indeed *cannot* be dull.

6

LOVE'S DISCIPLINE OUTWITS INCOMPATIBILITY

> Men have different gifts, but it is the same Spirit who gives
> them. There are different ways of serving God, but it is the
> same Lord who is served. God works through different men
> in different ways, but it is the same God who achieves His
> purposes through them all. Each man is given his gift by the
> Spirit that he may use it for the common good. (I Corinthians
> 12:4-7, Phillips).

One day after a meeting in Tennessee a nice young
man came up to me and asked rather abruptly, "Do towels
have to be hung all together on the wash line?" Instead of
answering I asked, "Are you a Southerner married to a
woman from Pennsylvania?" "How did you know?" he
replied. I told him my mother was from Pennsylvania
and my father was from Virginia and so I knew about
towels on a wash line!

Then he told me his wife was ill and he wanted to help
all he could, so he hung the wash on the line for her, but
she complained because he hung up the clothes as they
came from the basket. He couldn't see any sense in her
complaint. Teasing him I said, "It wouldn't hurt you to
hang the towels together to please her, would it?" He
laughed. So at least his irritation was gone!

G. K. Chesterton said he had known many happy mar-
riages but never a compatible one. *Incompatibility*:
grounds for divorce! The dictionary says, "Incapable of
existing together in harmony." *Incapability* is the word
nearer the truth — it is *plain failure in human relations*.
It is not the difference in persons that causes the incompatibility but the attitude toward those differences.

A bride of only a few months went out to a public
telephone one early morning to complain to me of her
bridegroom. She spit out her anger: "When we go to
bed, Jim wants to read before he goes to sleep and I want
to talk. I am so mad at him I could knock his teeth out!"

54

(And she was a prayer group leader!) The window open or shut at night, bathroom towels, the bedroom heated or cold, and hundreds of other different habits enter into marriage. These are post-wedding revelations. They are small things that get magnified out of all proportion when one or two people lose the proper sense of values.

One woman had a husband whose mother had always picked up after him. Of course, he expected the same of his wife. When he came home he dropped his hat at the door, threw his coat over a chair, and other things at any convenient spot as he went along. His wife could always find where he was by following the trail. She got tired of hanging his things up for him, so one day she gathered everything together and made a dummy on the kitchen floor. Later when he looked in the closet for his coat, it wasn't there. He called his wife and she took him to the "man" lying on the kitchen floor. Fortunately he had a sense of humor. He said, "Why, the poor man! What's wrong with him?" She replied, "He has the dropsy!" That took care of the dropsy *and* the possible incompatibility.

My little, big awakening was: he wanted his feet thoroughly wrapped at night and I wanted my shoulders covered! Extra size sheets took care of that! One marriage almost broke up over sticky oil cloth on the breakfast table. Keeping up with active children and their jelly bread kept that mother going. When she realized what an irritation this "sweetness" was to her husband she was more careful about cleaning up.

Radio and TV can become even bigger barriers. If she wants classical music and he wants pop music there may be real discord. In the early days of one radio to a house one woman kept a music station on all day. As soon as her husband came home he turned off her station and turned to the news. She'd come along and turn off his news to get her music again. Later they went to a spiritual conference and came home changed people. After that when he came home she turned the radio to the news. When he realized what she had done he turned the radio back to the music for her. If they hadn't laughed they might have landed into the old conflict again in their efforts to be kind to each other!

I like Ogden Nash's definition of marriage. After his rhymes on reasons for differences in marriage he adds,

> That is why marriage is so much more interesting than divorce,
> Because it's the only known example of the happy meeting of the immovable object and the irresistible force.
> So I hope that husbands and wives will continue to debate and combat over everything debatable and combatable,
> Because I believe a little incompatibility is the spice of life, particularly if he has the income and she is pattable.[1]

The old nursery rhyme goes even farther in the solution of differences:

> Jack Spratt could eat no fat,
> His wife could eat no lean,
> So between them both, you see,
> They licked the platter clean.

Many differences can be made to fit together to make a whole. I remember the young minister who was very disorganized in his own life. Then he married a girl who was a trained secretary and a model of efficiency. He let her help him get organized and she said he helped her to be more gracious to people. They complemented each other and so made a whole couple.

In the very years when it was said that "opposites attract," the books emphasized *togetherness* — a couple must go everywhere together and do everything together. In the name of togetherness the men got caught in the dishwashing routine. (One reason for so many electric dishwashers today!) Women had to bowl, play golf and go deep sea fishing, no matter how seasick they got. Many times the physical togetherness put a strain on the inner togetherness.

In those days of emphasis on togetherness a single girl came to me and said, "Last night some of us girls over at the Seminary were wondering about you and your hus-

---

[1] "I Do, I Will, I Have," *Verses from 1929 on* (Boston: Little, Brown & Co., 1959).

band. We seldom see you going places together." I answered, "Listen, my dear, my husband would be bored going with me to the opera. When the coloratura goes into action, he would laugh! Why should I have him bored and the music spoiled for me? I can't understand what goes on in some of his scientific meetings so he'd just as soon go alone. But you go tell the girls that a lot of couples who are always seen together in public life live separately at home. Baxter and I share a double bed."

One can do more than accept differences — they can be appreciated. It is marriage murder to depreciate or belittle another's interest. I was in a minister's home where the husband's hobby was the collection of antiques. As he got around the country he kept his eyes open and had an excellent opportunity to find rare pieces from glass ware to grandfather clocks and beds. He brought them home and made what repairs were necessary and then sold them to augment his meager church salary. The garage was full and cupboards and stray chairs and tables stood in every room in the house. His wife kept house around them or incorporated them into her decorating scheme. She was an excellent housekeeper; she was also an excellent wife. She made room for joy in her husband's hobby.

We have already seen that possessive love is selfish and it is questionable as to whether it can be called real love. Paul Ramsey's statement is pertinent, " 'I love you' may simply mean 'I love *me* and I *want* you.' " The mature love that can make any marriage a success no matter what the differences are is a giving-love that gives full freedom to each partner to grow in his own special interests and abilities.

The friend (see Chapter 1) who told me about her parents loving each other through all differences wrote me further:

> In our family we learned very early that people could disagree and still have an underlying acceptance of one another. I think we were "old world" in the sense that we were all sort of lusty about life. When the folks were in conflict they neither

tried to hide it or to restrain themselves for the sake of their children. Very early I learned that adults had some dimension of understanding that I couldn't quite fathom. I grew up in the depression and most of their conflict was about money.

One winter evening we were sitting around the dining room table. Our only light was from an oil lamp, the lights had been turned off because of the unpaid electric bill. A bitter argument arose between my parents and my mother got up, put on her coat, and stormed out into the darkness. Dad followed immediately. I felt like my world had collapsed but my teenage sisters went on nonchalantly clearing the table. What seemed like hours later I heard blessed footsteps on the porch. There they were coming in out of the darkness, their arms around each other — and laughing! This was a lesson to me — that conflict did not mean the end.

On his last Mother's Day gift to Mother, Dad had inscribed, 'Sweetheart, Wife, Mother, Grandmother, Companion, and the best Pal a man ever had'."

A compassionate understanding of the weaknesses of another is an integral and redemptive part of true love. This love is patience, a patience which eliminates any remembrance of thoughtless words spoken under strain. It is the love that can stand the strain of tension without breaking.

We need to say it again that it is not incompatibility that is the real trouble in any marriage but the attitude toward incompatibility. But this attitude may have become an emotional stickler — an obsession. It sounds almost like a platitude to say that love will change a wrong attitude. But anyone who is wise enough in the midst of helplessness to turn to the God of love for mercy, change and understanding will find the beginning of new attitudes.

It is a blessing that we are not left to handle these emotions alone. Self-control is an integral part of the given fruit of the Spirit, with love, patience, kindness, gentleness. (Galatians 5:22, 23) Accepting one's helplessness before an obsessive emotion is the initial step toward looking to God for His gracious help.

The emotional attitude that we want to be rid of is really the hardness of unforgiveness. It is voiced in "Why did I marry this person? How did I ever get caught in this mess? I can't take it any more." Unforgiveness means we are thinking from our own standpoint and what we are getting out of this marriage. Unforgiveness means we have lost love — for God, for others and for ourselves.

After accepting the fact of one's own helplessness, the next step in the discipline of love is gratitude. I remember so often what Genie Price said: "*Ingratitude* snaps shut the human heart. Grateful hearts are always open hearts. They are hearts which have received. Even God cannot squeeze a blessing through a closed heart."[2]

After thanking God for His available help it should be an exciting adventure to list the *good* things about your mate. What did you appreciate before you got so irritated? Then you can also figure out the reasons in his life (or hers) why he has these irritating habits. The careless wife may have had a mother who was a perfectionist. Other habits may be leftovers from childhood patterns or teen-age rebellions. The one who is seeking the way through these difficulties is the one who must set the other one free to find his way out of immature ways. (And it will never help to tell him he is immature!) You cannot set him free until his good points mean the most to you.

As one looks to God and His love and looks with understanding to his mate, lo! that unforgiving hard attitude has melted away and a deeper love has taken its place.

And what has your teen-age audience seen? What have they learned? They learn what you learn. Is it the way through difficulties with God's help no matter what the strain? If you work it out with each other the teen-ager will know also that his differences with you will never break his relationship with you. This is a security that parents and God alone can give.

---

[2] *A Woman's Choice* (Grand Rapids, Mich.: Zondervan Publishing House, 1962), p. 28.

7

LOVE'S DISCIPLINE FINDS NEW CHANNELS OUT OF LONELINESS

Be still and know that I am God. (Psalm 46:10)

As long as thou livest thou art subject to change, even against thy will; so that thou art at one time merry, at another sad; at one time quiet, at another troubled; now devout, now undevout; now diligent, now listless; now grave, now light minded.

But he that is wise and well instructed in spirit standeth fast upon these changing things, not heeding what he feeleth in himself or which way the wind bloweth; but that the whole intent of his mind may be to the right and the best end. . . . And the purer the eye of the intention is, with so much the more constancy doth a man pass through the several kinds of storms which assail him. (*The Imitation of Christ*)[1]

Loneliness has nothing to do with being *alone*. The greatest loneliness on earth is to know one's self as being separated from God. This is not only loneliness but *lostness*. The only way out of this loneliness is to be still, be honest, be obedient to the God of love whose love is measured by the Cross. The saving grace of Christ will take care of that lostness. With Him one is never alone.

The next kind of loneliness is a loneliness in the midst of people with whom one cannot communicate. And this communication has little to do with talk. We live in a talkative world, a world that is afraid of silence because silence reveals emptiness and lostness. People talk, talk to cover up emptiness, and even to cover up the inability to communicate.

The greatest experiences of joy and sorrow take place beyond the spoken word. The deepest communication is between those who know and trust each other. This kind of communication helps us to understand the communication between God and man.

---

[1]Chapter 33, The Macmillan Company, 1934.

It is often said that everybody talks and no one listens. This is the relationship many people have with God — they do all the talking to God and no listening and call it prayer. They might just as well use a Tibetan prayer wheel and save their time for something else. Greater than the communication between the aquanauts at the bottom of the sea and the astronauts out in space is the communication anyone can have with the Creator of all who is our Heavenly Father. This communication begins on God's side; He reaches out to us before we ever turn to Him. This is the reason we must learn to be still to know Him. Then we learn to speak with Him.

Real communication with other persons must begin the same way. We must be able to listen. This is practicing giving-love because we are learning to begin our thinking from the side of the other person.

It is hard for some people to communicate with words. To push them to words may only create a self-consciousness that will close the door to the deeper kind of communication which might otherwise have been possible. Thank God for people who have the gift of silence untainted by self-consciousness. They may be used of God as His listening ear.

People who are free from the compulsion to talk are often the ones with words of wisdom when the compulsive talkers turn speechless. Believe it or not, this last year a man brought his wife to a conference so she would learn to talk more! She listened and smiled with understanding and with a minimum of words she was a full member of the group. When she spoke on the last day she was worth listening to. I thought of the good fortune of her children who had a mother who didn't talk them to distraction.

It has been said that the lack of ability to communicate is the greatest difficulty in marriage. If you have found yourself in the heartbreaking loneliness of living with another when all avenues of communication seem to be closed, you know a great human helplessness. Self-pity will lock and bar the already closed doors to communication. You cannot really compensate for this loneliness either.

If you lavish undue attention on your children you will only hurt your children. If you turn to outside interests, you still have to return "home" to dead silence. Escape is not the way out of this loneliness.

You are fortunate if your doors of communication have not been closed long, for when silence is a barrier between two people the chasm should be bridged as quickly as possible. It is too easy to overestimate such loneliness, but delay is really dangerous.

How did the doors close? Did they slam shut or close so quietly you did not see it happen? Did he have his feelings hurt and withdraw and did you withdraw in retaliation? Or did the doors close from neglect because of too much attention given to the new baby or to the work outside the home?

The first one to sense the rising barrier is the one responsible for taking the initiative in reconciliation. I wonder if there is anything that requires more maturity than to be the first one to take steps toward reconciliation, the first one to say, "I am sorry, I was wrong." These words are so hard to speak. This is where a double bed counts! It is so much easier to reach out an arm as a gesture of reconciliation than it is to use words. Words sound stilted anyway and the touch of a hand is deeper communication than words can ever be. It is worth any sacrifice of foolish pride any time to do all possible to restore communication and real relationship as quickly as possible.

Renewed love seems greater than the original experience of love. I suppose it is because it has come through fire without being destroyed and it brings exultation of victory with it.

Bertha and Andrew were a couple who knew the meaning of their marriage vows when they took them. Lest they forget they added another vow between themselves and before God that they would never let night fall on any misunderstanding between them. This love discipline they kept throughout their married life and through all their years of service in India. They were truly one in Christ.

Then Andrew met an untimely death and Bertha faced this tragedy alone with her five children in a foreign land. But she was prepared — because she loved God and her husband. As she sat by his bed in his last hours — midnight hours — she felt she could not face this loss. But she turned to the Father of love and He answered her heart's cry. As her husband's life slipped away, a great light seemed to appear above his body and Bertha knew the Presence of Christ as she had never known it before. Even for this He was adequate. From that hour on she never knew loneliness. What everyone thought would be lonely agony for her evolved into the richest ministry of her life.

Before this experience Bertha might have been called "just a housewife and mother" and a "good Christian," but after this she was in God's kingdom what the young people in camp christened her: "Princess." Her presence anywhere seemed to bring the power and love of God into any situation. One day on a train going west the conductor came through her car as if he were looking for some one. He stopped in front of Bertha and said, "You look like you could help. Will you please come over into a first class drawing room for the rest of the journey to help a Hollywood actress who is in great distress?" Bertha went and before they reached their destination the actress had accepted the Christ Bertha loved so much.

Is your loneliness that of being bereft of a partner who was very dear to you? Then thank God for good memories. Take courage from what God did for Bertha. His promises are for adequate help in any need. God can even use your loss as a means of helping others. "Blessed be the God and Father of our Lord Jesus Christ, the Father of mercies, and God of all comfort, who comforts us in all our affliction, so that we may be able to comfort those who are in any affliction, with the comfort with which we ourselves are comforted by God" (II Corinthians 1:3, 4).

Then there is the possible loneliness that may come when only one is ready to accept the Lord as Saviour. Will this bring separation in understanding from a loved mate?

But it is a greater love for this mate if the living Lord be brought into the marriage, even in this partial way.

The early Christians faced this same matter. Paul wrote to the Corinthians, "For the unbelieving husband is consecrated through his wife, and the unbelieving wife is consecrated through her husband. . . . Wife, how do you know whether you will save your husband? Husband, how do you know whether you will save your wife?" (I Corinthians 7:14, 16). Others were advised to live in such a way that the non-Christian would be won by his mate's life even without the necessity of *words* of witness (I Peter 3:1, 2).

It seems that this experience happens to women more than men. Mothers especially who stand alone with God are tempted to feel self-pity because they have to take the religious leadership in the family with the children. If the spiritually weak husband is sensitive about his "headship" in the family she may have a very ticklish situation. But self-pity will never help. It must be avoided like poison, for it is poison to one's faith — and love. God has no part in arrogance, impatience or irritation. His love working in one person gives God a chance with anyone who doesn't know Him.

Then there is the loneliness of parents when the last child leaves home. If their need-love never matured they will indeed be lonely. One such mother, a minister's wife said she couldn't stand it. Then when she became a widow she moved in with her younger daughter. This daughter was overpowered by her "good" mother who never saw what she did to her own daughter. In the name of "unselfish helpfulness" mother took charge of daughter, house, kitchen, buying and everything. She was so blinded by her own image of herself as an "unselfish mother" that she broke her daughter's spirit. Of course she blamed everything on her son-in-law whom she despised. Because of her attitude toward him her daughter was thrown constantly into a conflict of loyalties.

If an older sister had not stepped in with drastic measures, only God knows what might have happened. Friends had to help the sisters know they had no reason for guilt for what they had to do. The dear woman's need-love had not found satisfaction in God, so it was perverted in relation to her children. She was not helping her daughter, she was trying to escape from her loneliness. She would have had no need for escape if she had kept her relation to Christ truly alive and growing.

Some old people complain about being unwanted. There may be more reason than the selfishness of younger relatives. I am convinced that the problem of "old age" is *not age but selfishness*. Some people left alone are so bitter that anyone feels poisoned by a few minutes in their presence. This need not be. God is not dead. The greater the need, the more abundant is the grace of God to meet that need.

My "star saint" was Miss Densie. Her initials were D.E.H. A friend said one time her initials meant *Delightfully Enjoying Him*. She belongs to this book even though she was never married, for she conquered loneliness all her life. She was my teacher in my teen years and I could never forget her. I found her again after many years in a home for the aged. They told me that she was the saint of the home. The last time I saw her was three weeks before she died of cancer. I was shocked at her appearance, but amazed at the glory on her face in spite of her intense suffering. As soon as she saw me she exclaimed, "Oh, Anna, I am so glad you have come. I wanted to tell you once again to tell everyone that Jesus is alive. And I am going to be with Him very soon." I could not help but say, "Oh, Miss Densie, that is wonderful."

She gave me a list she had made of assets in later life. Here is her answer to loneliness:

1. Our afflictions work inner glory as we near God's eternal things.
2. Our eyes become more keen for the unseen than for the seen and we have a clearer vision of the everlasting world.
3. Our faith-walk is stronger, and we can better roam the wide world in prayer.
4. We can see now that this is the part of life for which the first was made, "and we see the light of God's eternity piercing the storm clouds of our darkest days."

5. We have learned that "in His will is our peace."
6. Though my mind is perturbed at times, my heart is yet at peace, for I know that I do not have an eternal abiding place here, but an "inheritance incorruptible, undefiled, and that never fades away, reserved in heaven . . ."
7. The night is almost gone, and the day breaks with a light that reveals unexpected beauties in death. A funeral becomes a coronation in Christ.
8. Life is still an adventure, and we are nearing the peak, maybe achieving some eternal gain for the universe and God's great plan.
9. "Peace does not mean the end of all our striving;
   Joy does not mean the drying of our tears.
   Peace is the power that comes to souls arriving
   Up to the Light where God Himself appears."
   —*Studdert Kennedy*
10. "There is a beauty about age which the beauty of youth cannot imitate or duplicate." —*R. Smith*
11. "It is the will that sets the mileage limits
   It is the heart that spans the skies."
12. "You better hurry and grow older; you don't know what you are missing. I am having the best time of my life. God is giving me some of the greatest thoughts I ever had."
   —*A. C. Wieand*

One of the tragedies of Western living is the compartmentalization of age groups. Every age has something to give to every other age. But when young people are thrown with older people it is often in too close quarters, physically and psychologically. They do not find out about the grace, beauty and wisdom of age but only the irritation at teen-age ways.

If you have loneliness and conquer it, your courage and bravery will be a great challenge to your children and grandchildren. They will learn with you that *whether I feel it or not, He is here. I can walk in faith with full hope in His unlimited love.*

8

LOVE DISCIPLINED GROWS
THROUGH HARDSHIP

> This priceless treasure we hold, so to speak, in a common earthenware jar — to show that the splendid power of it belongs to God and not to us. We are handicapped on all sides but we are never frustrated; we are puzzled, but never in despair. We are persecuted, but we never have to stand it alone: we may be knocked down but we are never knocked out!
>
> (II Corinthians 4:7-9, Phillips)

Promising undying love during courtship days is the usual experience of all lovers. We need not question the honesty of this promise. The problem is: why is the promised love counted as unreliable as soon as the hazards of daily life together appear?

Perhaps the answer is in Count Herman Keyserling's words:

> The real cause of the failure in marriage in western lands is that we expect it to be happy. If we could only learn to contemplate marriage, not as an instrument of unalloyed bliss, but as a means to the realization of personality, with all the suffering and sacrifice that it involves, we should be better prepared to reap its full rewards.

This should be easier for Christians who commit their lives to God at any cost. ("Were the whole world of nature mine, that were a present far too small . . . .") But even many Christians think of the Christian life as one of joy only. I know a very joyous Christian who married late in life. She had prayed much about this marriage before she took the step. Then she ran into some hard disappointments. Two questions shook her faith: Did she miss in her guidance? Why did God let her joy be taken away? She is learning the suffering one can do for another and also that the Resurrection follows the dark days of the Cross.

The modern Church has often failed by giving people the idea that everything will be smooth and easy. It is true the burden is light, but there is no promise that there will be no burden. And Christian joy is sometimes in spite of difficulties. *Blessed* are those who mourn and *blessed* are those persecuted for righteousness' sake (Matthew 5:1-12). Jesus endured the cross for the joy that was beyond the cross (Hebrew 12:2).

Church youth leaders often try merely to make youth happy and to make church life as appealing as secular interests. They lose in the competition because they appeal to the wrong motive. I am ashamed to *beg* people to come to church. There is a need for coming, but that need is not met by mere entertainment appeals.

Our government has been wiser than some church people. Youth are challenged in the Peace Corps advertisements: "You are going to be right in there with monotony, illiteracy and an army of bloodthirsty mosquitoes. You're going to work sixteen hours a day . . . and you will see one fraction of the results you'd hoped for. . . ." With that call, very little pay and the provision to live like the poor and underprivileged people of forty-eight countries, our American youth responded by the thousands. And many have returned for a second term of the same thing. They really don't ask for an easy life, but only for the courage to live it.

Perhaps it is difficult to be conditioned to meet the hard things of life when our way of living is so air-conditioned and so filled with comforts and labor-saving devices. There are still many people who remember the Depression. It has been said that a depression is a time when we have to do without the things our parents never had. But expectations have changed also. People don't start at the bottom any more. A cup and saucer of a bride's chosen dinnerware pattern may cost as much as her grandmother's whole set of dishes.

Too many times the abundance of *things* a child receives is a substitute for relationship and love. But nearly all American children get what they want, by some means or other. Very few are really conditioned for the hardships they may have to face later. Neither have they learned the disciplines of relationship and love.

68

Parents who cannot go through hardship together, who cannot find solutions for their personal difficulties are losing the respect of their teen-agers at the very time when adolescents need courage for their daily and future uncertainties.

Parents and children are prepared for the days when everything is easy, but they are not prepared for the crises of life. When the way is hard they lose courage and shrink back. But the divine appraisal is "If he shrinks back, my soul has no pleasure in him" (Hebrews 10:38). Perhaps this all began when the little ones first tried to climb the stairs and mother held them back for *fear* they would hurt themselves. So the child finally gave up and lost the zest for conquering hard things. The dropouts in school *and* life are part of this sad story.

There are unnecessary hardships which come because one partner is immature. These are the hardest to deal with. A young wife found a deep fear growing in her at the time of her husband's return each evening. He was a perfectionist and would look into the sink to see if any dirty dishes were left, look into the cupboard to see if all was in order. Once he found some good china unwashed in the sink and he broke every piece. Her fear grew and broke her courage for living until she could not keep from crying most of the time. Then he was irritated by her crying. Didn't he give her everything? Finally he took her to the hospital for a "nervous breakdown." As they entered the hospital doors her latent humor got the best of her and she asked him, "Who is entering the hospital — you or I?"

This is like the experience of Dr. Robert J. McAllister, a psychiatrist writing in *Marriage: A Psychological and Moral Approach.*[1]

> The only thing which troubles me is that the individual making the referral often sends me the wrong marital partner. I am asked to see the alcoholic husband whose charming wife, by her subtle sarcasm and her devious domination, gives him no

---

[1] Wm. C. Bier, S.J. ed. (New York: Fordham University Press, 1965), p. 186.

peace at home, or more truly, not even a home. I am asked to see the promiscuous wife whose deeply religious husband, by his rigidity and ritualism, makes her feel cheap if she enjoys sex and guilty if she enjoys life.

Neurotic and psychotic people need professional help, but in the meantime it is always helpful if one partner knows the love of God and can accept the discipline of love so that he can see the other partner in his true condition and not be conquered by crushing despair. This takes the courage that only God can give.

Infidelity is the hardest for a good man or a good woman to forgive in a mate. When it comes to hardship this is concentrated sorrow. If the "innocent" party finds it out, the first reaction after the first shock is usually condemnation. But that doesn't help one already full of guilt. Even with a promise of change the "innocent" one is tempted to constant suspicion and continued policing.

If it is the husband who has failed, you, the wife, still have the inside track. Your are the mother of his children. You have the memories with him of a better day. He does not have to be furtive to be with you as he does with the other woman. But, if you go around weeping all the time and feeling sorry for yourself, you hand him to the other woman on a silver platter. One woman who had almost done this turned to God for help in time. All tears left her, she quit blaming or policing or asking questions. She left him free to answer to God, not to her. She could pray with him and he with her that this thing which possessed him would leave. She wrote, "Last night he said to me, 'You have been so beautiful to me . . . I haven't seen a worried look cross your face in a week. That's quite an accomplishment for God.' This has been like a week of resurrection."

It is strange that Jesus was more merciful toward those who fell into this sin than any other. He forgave so mercifully and said, "Sin no more." The gratitude that comes from real forgiveness to a guilty person is so deep it cannot be spoken. A wife who had betrayed her husband told him he had a right to leave her even though her "affair" was over. He said he could not leave her because he loved her. And he wanted to be around when she came into the fullness of the consciousness of guilt so he could help her know how great is the forgiveness of God. And he was there when that hour came.

These are griefs worse than death. But death, too, often untimely, comes to every family. Giving in to grief may become a real sickness; nevertheless any normal person has real sorrow at the loss of a loved one. Such a sorrow can do much to bring the rest of the family much closer together as they find their comfort in God "Blessed are they that mourn for they shall be comforted."

There are all kinds of other hardships that can come to a family, among them financial reverses. Often parents will be more concerned because of the children. But when the family faces trouble together the teen-agers are as brave as anyone. I still feel inspired by the family I wrote about in *Going Steady with God* (p. 202). The father lost his business during the Second World War through no fault of his own. For a while it looked like they had lost everything else, including the old family home. The whole community was heartsick for them. A neighbor met the teen-age son on the street and asked, "What on earth are you going to do now?" The boy answered, "We are going to practice the faith we've been professing all our lives." That's the stuff of youth. And we must not forget it.

God uses all hardships that come to us — if we let Him.

God corrects us all our days for our own benefit, to teach us his holiness. Now obviously no "chastening" seems pleasant at the time: it is in fact most unpleasant. Yet when it is all over we can see that it has quietly produced the fruit of real goodness in the characters of those who have accepted it in the right spirit. So tighten your loosening grip and steady your wavering hand. Don't wander away from the path but forge steadily onward. On the right path the limping foot recovers strength and does not collapse. (Hebrews 12:10-13; Phillips)

9

LOVE'S RESTORATIVE POWER — EVEN FOR THE HOPELESS

It has been said that there is only one step between failure and success — quitting. People try all the *human* ways to save a marriage and then they give up all hope. This is not a new experience even for the people called God's people. In the time of the prophet Ezekiel the people had become utterly hopeless, so a message came to Ezekiel — a graveyard drama:

> The hand of the Lord was upon me, and carried me out in the spirit of the Lord, and set me down in the midst of the valley which was full of bones, and caused me to pass by them round about: and, behold, there were very many in the open valley; and, lo, they were very dry. And he said unto me, Son of man, can these bones live? And I answered, O Lord God, thou knowest. Again he said unto me, Prophesy upon these bones, and say unto them, O ye dry bones, hear the word of the Lord. . . . Behold I will cause breath to enter into you, and ye shall live. . . . So I prophesied as he commanded . . . and the breath came into them, and they lived. . . .
> (Ezekiel 37:1-5, 10, KJ)

Is your marriage one of wasted years, disillusioned hopes, deadness? Is this the mess your life is in? Are you sitting down in a modern valley of dry bones? Do you think there is no hope for you? Are you candidates for the column, "Can this marriage be saved?" Are you really spiritually dead even though you are active in your church? There is not only hope for you, but a promise from the days of the prophet that God can even use your wasted years and restore them to your satisfaction and God's praise:

> And I will restore to you the years that the locust hath eaten. . . . And ye shall eat in plenty, and be satisfied, and praise the name of the Lord your God. . . . And ye shall know . . . that I am the Lord your God. . . .
> And it shall come to pass afterward, that I will pour out my spirit upon all flesh; and your sons and your daughters shall

> prophesy, your old men shall dream dreams, your young men
> shall see visions. . . . And it shall come to pass, that whosoever
> shall call on the name of the Lord shall be delivered. . . .
>
> (Joel 2:25-28, 32 KJ)

These messages of hope from the Lord through the prophets came when the people were in the most hopeless situations. But in spite of the proffered hope from the Lord very few people accepted the mercy and love offered by God. So the Son of God had to come to live among men, to *live* the Word from God. He was tempted in all points as we are. (Hebrews 4:15) He faced the hazards of daily living and the tests of every crisis with unbroken love. Of course, they murdered Him as they had murdered the prophets, but His Cross revealed the depth of His love — of God's love — a love that has no limits. Through His Cross every follower of the Saviour may now be under the control of that same love (II Corinthians 5:14).

How dare we act hopeless when the power of the Holy Spirit is now available to each one of us for every need? Listen:

> . . . and how tremendous is the power available to us who be-
> lieve in God. That power is the same divine energy which
> was demonstrated in Christ when he raised him from the dead.
> . . . To you, who were spiritually dead all the time that you
> drifted along on the stream of this world's ideas of living, . . .
> to you Christ has given life! (Ephesians 1:19, 20; 2:1, 2)

I believe God means what He says in His Word. The greatest challenge we face is to accept His love and power for our own lives.

So, in the light of His offered power for each one of us, look again at the "hopeless" mess you are in. Perhaps you and your mate are merely living parallel lives, each going his own way without any remnant of interest in each other. Or are you in constant competition and conflict with each other? Are all your energies taken up in outwitting each other? Perhaps you live in fear of your mate's spasmodically cruel tongue or tyrannical actions. Do you let despair blast every renewal of hope for a better life together?

There are many sad stories. One husband was legalistic and demanding, but in spite of his church life, whenever he went out with the boys he came home tipsy. This was more than his wife could take. In her distaste she withdrew from him and days of bitterness always followed. Another man came to marriage with very little personal security. His capable wife did not know how to give him the security he needed, but began to despise and ridicule him until he lost what courage he did have. It seemed that all the possibilities of his life "died aborning." Is it too late for these people?

Another couple love each other in spite of the fact that they are both married to other people. They are helpless before this obsession, even though they want to do God's will. Why don't they accept the discipline of a deeper, purer love? Is there hope for them?

Whenever a little hope stirs the waters for the people caught in the meshes of emotion and despair they reach out for help, but so many of them fall back into human helplessness again. One feels like crying out with the prophet. "Hast thou not known? hast thou not heard, that the everlasting God, the Lord, the Creator of the ends of the earth, fainteth not, neither is weary? . . . He giveth power to the faint; and to them that have no might he increases strength" (Isaiah 40:28, 29 KJ).

So — would you really like to get out of the mess you are in? If you would you will have to take the life and teaching of Jesus at face value. You will have to accept at the very beginning that, no matter how justified you are in your grievances, the way out is never in a fight for your "rights." Christ's suffering was *for others* and never because they hurt Him. You will have to eliminate all self-pity, all blaming of other people. You will have to think yourself into your mate's place and find out how to help him find fulfillment and happiness. If you do this with God's help you will find distinctive opportunity to test the truth of the Good News (Gospel) that came to us through the Cross of our Lord Jesus Christ.

Looking at this Christ-love as portrayed on the Cross while one is in the midst of conflict and despair in human relationships is a different matter from the holy consideration of the same truth in a three-hour Good Friday service in the most beautiful Church in town. When we live through the tragedy we do not have beautiful organ music in the background; neither did He when He suffered for us. He had only His faith in God's unfailing love.

Christians who act competitively in self-defense are still living in the Old Testament. For them it is still "an eye for an eye and a tooth for a tooth." But Jesus went much farther in the advancement of human relations. He said, "But what I tell you is this: Do not set yourself against the man who wrongs you. If someone slaps you on the right cheek, turn and offer him your left. If a man wants to sue you for your shirt, let him have your coat as well. If a man in authority makes you go one mile, go with him two! Give when you are asked to give; and do not turn your back on a man who wants to borrow" (Matthew 5:38-42, NEB).

Most people either ignore what Jesus was saying or they follow it legalistically and imitatively. They miss the very point he was making. He wasn't talking about laws as such, but about restoring relationships. They are more like the boy who was always getting into fights. His mother told him to count to a hundred whenever he was tempted to fight. That evening he came home with a black eye. His mother asked him if he had counted to a hundred. He said, "Yes, this is what I got while I was counting. But you ought to see what I did to Bill after I finished counting!"

Jesus was saying something greater than suggesting a mere passive acceptance of another's aggressive act. Mere passive acceptance would really do harm to the aggressive one. Jesus wanted to break the static relationship which led to the vicious circle of cumulative retaliation. Jesus always worked on the basis of creatively improving relationship. Perhaps the easiest one of Jesus' illustrations for us to understand is the one about going the second mile. A Roman soldier in an occupied country could command the service of any man of the country to carry his luggage for one mile. Then he had to release this man and force the service of another man. Imagine his surprise if a man at the end of the forced mile of service would say, "I'll carry it another mile for you."

That second mile is the breakthrough into another plane of dynamic relationship. Dr. S. I. McMillen has discussed the vicious cycle or chain reaction of destructive attitudes in the family under stress.[1] But he says,

> . . . such heartbreaking disease-producing reactions can be stopped by any member who will accept the role of a scapegoat. The whole family can be salvaged if one member breaks the chain by giving up his right to have his rights. Because a mother loves much, she is often the one who saves the whole family by sacrificing herself and her rights. . . .
>
> Thus a person who is following the Lord Jesus Christ is able to break vicious reactions within a family. There is a universal and powerful draw in hands with nail prints. Calvary gives motivation that psychiatry and counseling cannot provide.
>
> As Sadler (Dr. Wm.) said, "Some day our . . . scientific development . . . may catch up with the teaching of this Man of Galilee."

Many people are satisfied to think of marriage as a 50-50 proposition or as mere "give and take." But 50-50 leads to policing each other to see that the balance is kept, or else one does all the giving and the other all the taking. To avoid the hazards of policing each other, one person must run the risk of lowering his guard and be willing to go 150. This is going the second mile. It always looks like such a perilous step before one takes it, but the second mile is never servitude — it is service in freedom. In the second mile one finds courage that is synonymous with real personal dignity.

Suppose you are in a mess with your mate and you think *it* is hopeless, *he* is hopeless, or *she* is hopeless. Why not try Jesus' law for restoring relationships? You have no love any more? That doesn't matter. Try the mechanics of love anyway. You can at least start with that. Look at your mate. He hurt you, yes, but why did he want to hurt you? Think back to the days when you vowed love for

---

[1]"How to Avoid Family Problems," *Christian Life*, January, 1966.

each other. How did you get off the track? Perhaps disillusionments came because you expected only orchids out of life and you did not know how to face reality. But no matter how you missed the way and what "unforgivable" things have happened, you can do no more than start from where you are today.

To clear the present, so that it is not clouded by the past, forgiveness must take place. The most immediate block to forgiveness is self-pity. Self-pity is self-centeredness. Self-centeredness or egocentricity is "condensed darkness."[2] Self-pity always brings a black mood, a sense of darkness. Only the light of God's forgiving love can dispel this darkness. We need God's forgiveness. He always gives it but we cannot receive it until we forgive others. It is almost frightening to remember how casually we have all prayed together, "Forgive us *as we forgive*."

Jesus always insisted on the need for forgiveness in all human relations. Even our religious worship is of no value without it. "So that if, while you are offering your gift at the altar, you should remember that your brother has something against you, you must leave your gift there before the altar and go away. Make your peace with your brother first, then come and offer your gift" (Matthew 5:23, Phillips). When the "brother" is one's mate, reconciliation is even more important, but more difficult. In this case you go to confess your own failure. But if he has wronged you, again you must take the initiative for reconciliation. You go, not to blame, but to win him. "If your brother wrongs you, go and have it out with him at once — just between the two of you. If he will listen to you, you have won him back as your brother" — or your mate! — (Matthew 18:15, Phillips). Again, reconciliation is more important between husband and wife than it is between "brothers." So whether your mate has wronged you or you have wronged him, whichever one "wakes up" first must take the initiative toward reconcilia-

[2]Fritz Kunkel, *Creation Continues* (New York: Charles Scribner's Sons, 1947), p. 76.

tion. He who asks forgiveness first is the stronger, not the weaker.

Jesus suggested that if you fail in the first attempt you should take another along; if you fail then, take it to the church; and if you still fail to win the one who has wronged you, you begin all over again from the beginning — which is to pray. "And I tell you once more that if two of you on earth agree in asking for anything it will be granted to you by my Heavenly Father" (Matthew 18:19, Phillips).

Peter was there with Jesus. He just about caught the point. The Rabbis had said one should forgive three times and then he was free to retaliate. But Peter asked, "Master, how many times can my brother wrong me and I must forgive him? Would seven times be enough?" How generous he was! "No," Jesus replied, "Not seven times but seventy times seven!" (Matthew 18:21, 22, Phillips). This is not arithmetic of the head but of the heart.

One remarkable Christian woman found out how difficult this is in marriage. She thought she could not take her husband's faithlessness any longer, but one Easter time she had a new vision of God's love and eternal forgiveness so she was enabled to forgive until seventy times seven — without self-pity. The years passed and she has won. She is all her husband wants. Now he is ill and needs much care. The woman wrote recently, "I have a calm and a courage that I did not dream existed — the Lord is good! That which I would have labeled a burden is a privilege with abiding love."

Another enemy of forgiving love is the attempt to escape one's own responsibility by placing the blame on the other one. It is so much easier to see and confess another's sins than one's own. The other person's sins are out of bounds until one is himself in the love of God.

One woman kept an accusing finger pointed at her straying husband while she wept constantly. She was a woman of prayer but this recent discovery of her husband's affair had crushed her completely. Then she turned to God for help and was at last able to be objective. Her self-pitying tears stopped. She quit questioning and policing him. She took all wifely pressure off him and trusted him to the working of the Holy Spirit. When she became strong and sweet his rationalization for straying melted away. She was no longer a judge he had to answer to; now he saw himself in God's sight. He said, "The miracle in her life has convicted me. I cannot get away from it."

The hardest step to take is to go to the depths of God-love in asking nothing for one's self. This is the rare love which persists in spite of contempt, indifference and despair. There is nothing such love cannot face; there is no limit to its faith, its hope, its endurance" (I Corinthians 13:7). When we see such love we can begin to have an insight into the meaning of God's love for us which Jesus revealed in life and death.

This rare love is the gift of God to those who truly give up self. It is a gift, but it can only be received by those who are willing to learn, for it must be learned. It must be learned from someone who loves. Many people have never had a real chance to learn it properly. This love is even greater in unlovely conditions. If this love must be learned *after* marriage it is even more difficult, but it is never too late for God's love — if only one person will give God a chance.

The wife who quit her tearful self-pity found herself free in the love of God, but she said she could stay in this love only as long as she continued to *praise* God. This is the way it works. "The Lord is near; have no anxiety, but in everything make your requests known to God in prayer and petition *with thanksgiving*" (Philippians 4:6, NEB). We must accept the fact that it always hurts for self to die — and stay dead until there is more of God-consciousness than self-consciousness.

Those who risk the loss of self find that what they have really lost are illusions and delusions and what they have really found is a new sense of fulfillment and dignity. This is the discovery in life of the truth Jesus gave: "For whoever wishes to save his life will lose it, and whoever, for my sake, loses his life shall find it" (Matthew 16:25 *Twentieth Century*). In fact, this is the only way to find the abundant life which Jesus promised (John 10:10).

Giving up self is giving up "rights." The seeming injustice in this sacrifice is what makes it hurt. But a redeemed marriage, a restored relationship, will be doubly undergirded with love of God because of participation in that love to achieve it. In practicing this greater love one finds that in God's realm no one — nothing — is hopeless.

The "right to happiness" is the most alluring of all "rights." The justification can easily blind a Christian to the deeper love of God. I am thinking of a woman who married too young. The glamour of mere romance died away but she found a measure of satisfaction in her home and in her children. Then, unwittingly and unsought for she came into an experience of illicit love which made her feel that she had never been loved before. With this experience came helplessness, despair and guilt. Then as she prayed she found new depths in which to love and for the sake of two families, two sets of children she asked nothing for herself except *to be responsible in the love of God*. There is glory in her life now as she is learning for the first time to have real giving-love for her husband. The surprise to her is the sense of fulfillment that has come to her since she thought she gave up her "right to happiness."

Your despairs, your failures, your courage and your victories are all lived with your teen-agers as an audience. If you give up to hopelessness you break their courage for life, but if you can find hope in the midst of despair you will have insulated your adolescent against the hazards of shallow glamour. And respect for the real courage of a parent is the greatest deterrent to rebellion at the age when idealism should be the strongest. It is hard for young people to rebel when they are overcome with awe at your courage.

Your teen ager wants and wonders about love more than anything else. If you have found God's love and can give this love to your family you will be giving your child the greatest gift on earth. This love requires a daily discipline. The discipline is defined (I Corinthians 13) in Paul's devastatingly practical words:

I am patient and kind
I am not jealous or boastful;
I am not arrogant or rude.
I do not insist on my own way:
I am not irritable or resentful. (RSV)
I keep no score of wrongs;
I do not gloat over other men's sins,
I delight in the truth.
There is *nothing love cannot face, there is no limit to its faith, its hope, and its endurance.* (NEB)

10

LOVE'S OPEN DOOR TO LIFE FOR YOU AND YOUR TEEN-AGER

Many parents do very well with their children when they are small but run into real confusion with them as teen-agers. The chances are that too many parents have not matured in their own love for one another and they have thereby lost the secret of harmonious relationship — if indeed, they ever knew it. They are ill prepared to be a help to their adolescent offspring when they are as confused as the children.

Teen-agers need *love* and want to know about love more than anything else. Where are they to learn about love — from the movies and a sex-ridden culture? Where are they to learn about the relationship of the physical to the spiritual phases of love — from the biology class, where they will learn only the physical aspects of sex? Where are they to learn about what makes a good marriage — from a magazine column?

You, the parents, carry the first responsibility to *show* your teen-ager what genuine love is. Your differences and even your conflicts won't hurt him at all if he sees you resolve them. If you can maintain an unbroken relationship through whatever happens you will have given your child the greatest gift of life: courage — a courage which is an integral part of the security of love. Courage is the *faith* and *hope* with *love* of the abiding qualities of life.

Teens need *security*, but this security is not necessarily in things. The insurance ads are all right as far as they go, but they do not tell about the greater security. The greatest security is in *relationship*, in a relationship that does not change with circumstances. This includes a growing relationship with God, recognizable relationship between father and mother which is never broken even by differences and misunderstandings, and his own relationship with both parents which is never broken no matter what happens.

Within this security of relationship teens need *independence*, too, or they will never grow up. Often a small child is pushed to independence before he is ready, when some mild indulgence would not hurt him. It is hard for parents to wait until he can stand, walk, and talk. Then when he is a teen-ager and often wants more independence than he is ready to be responsible for, the parental attitude is reversed. Out of their fears the parents do not grant even the freedom an adolescent thinks he can handle. He does need *bonds*, but not *bondage*. The parents must be the first to distinguish between the two. "Smother love" is in the bondage category and it will, of course, lead to rebellion — and it should. If teen rebellion is against sudden over-protectiveness the parent must first look to himself to see if he has been unwise. Then the parent must consider how he can help to keep that rebellion from being negative and destructive.

In the teen years the growth struggle is toward *self-identity*. Parents who have found their own self-identity fulfilled through their love for God and for each other will be able to provide the needed security, the right checks, while at the same time they will be able to give the necessary freedom for the teen's individual development. A young mother who is trying to do this with her own children wrote recently about her relationship with her own mother: "My mother has done many things for me and she loves me in her own way, but she has never permitted me to be myself or anything different from what she wanted me to be. I could never share with her the part of me that was not nice." A mother can give birth to her child, but her involvement as the years go by is to guard her child's right to find his own identity. This is a thrilling adventure to the wise parent and never a cause for self-pity.

Teen-agers need *privacy*. No parent should feel rejected just because a bedroom door is closed on him. This desire for privacy should be honored, including things as personal as letters and diaries. The teen-ager needs this inner quiet so that he can learn to handle his adjustments to life. Fortunate is the teen-ager who knows how to turn to a Heavenly Father when he feels the need of this privacy. Then there is no danger that this seeking of privacy will be an escape from life, but only a time of strengthening for daily living.

The love of God is the greatest love of all. You cannot expect your church to teach your child fully about the love of God. The church is only the ally of the home for the spiritual nurturing of your child. It is his second place to learn about God but it cannot be a substitute for what the home should do. If father loves his wife the way Christ loves the Church and if mother loves her husband and subjects herself to his well-being in the Lord, children will grow up to know the Living Presence of the Lord in their lives as they knew Him in their homes.

Young people want to be loved, they want appreciation, but they bitterly resent *anxiety* in their parents. They want to *be trusted* and anxiety makes them feel they are not trusted. It is hard for them to understand parental concern, much less parental anxiety. In this day of frightening newspaper stories a parent cannot avoid having concern and he finds it very easy to be a prey to anxiety. Concern belongs to love but anxiety is fussiness to the teens. It is the nameless fears which create the anxiety. It seems sometimes that love creates some of the parent's fear, for without love there would be indifference. But still anxiety must be conquered if one would keep the respect of the teen-agers. It is only through the grace of God that one can have genuine concern without the panic of anxiety.

Young people also want *discipline*, even when they resent it. Parents need to remember that *disciples* only can be disciplined. By the time they are in their teens respect must be won, it cannot be forced. Most of the resentment against discipline is because parents are so undisciplined in their own lives. Again parents have to live it and then they don't need to demand it. In this, too, it is disciplined love that has to be lived, the love that is always more than mere sentiment.

The concern which comes from disciplined love is, of course, a real sense of mature responsibility. This involves the recognition of the proper proportion of sharing in responsibility by both parents and children. Much parental anxiety is the result of failure to help children grow in responsibility. Teen-agers want "freedom" whether they have learned to be responsible or not. Their parents are headed for anxiety compounded by guilt if they have failed to teach this responsibility. But even here there is hope in the love of God. If the failure is recognized and perhaps shared with the teen-ager, *the genuine concern may be shared too. It is never too late to start with a clean slate through God's forgiveness and His grace for new life.*

But there are times when the parent has done all he can, even in his faith in God, and still it seems there is no hope. There are many forces working upon the youth of our day, and parents often feel helpless before these dark forces. The best answer I know to such heartache is in the life of Starr Daily. When Starr was born his mother died. His father promised her that he would raise this son for the God she loved so much, but dark forces played upon the heart of this boy and he was ready for the underworld before he was in his teens.

Last summer I had the high privilege of being with Starr Daily for a week in a summer conference. One day he spoke on "Blessed are they that mourn for they shall be comforted." He told the story of his father whose love never failed through all the years his son spent in the underworld, and whose faith in God never failed.

Starr Daily said, "If someone disappoints your hopes in them and all your prayers for them, you mourn. And Jesus said, 'Blessed are you if you mourn after this fashion,' for He says you will be comforted. And I believe this is true. My mind races back over a chasm of many, many years to my childhood. My father had great hopes in me, he never lost faith in me. I had never known a word of condemnation to cross his lips for anything I did. And all my life, while he lived, he mourned. I never did anything that pleased him. All his prayers for me were unanswered. I went off into the underworld and there I lived for twenty-five years. He never lost his love for me, but he always mourned.

"I remember as a boy, ten years old, seeing him sitting in his rocking chair, by the old coal-burning stove, and his face had a strange sort of suffering in it, thinking about his desires and ambitions for me and all the ways I hurt him. He would sit there and mourn . . . . He never saw a single hope he had for me fulfilled. He spent a rather sizeable fortune trying to keep me out of trouble, and sometimes he would travel by train for long distances when I would write him a very crude postal card telling him I was in trouble again. Then he would come and try to get me out. One man told him: 'John, if that were my boy I'd just turn loose of him and let him go to hell.' And father said, 'But he's not your boy, he's mine!' That was the difference."

Starr continued, "My father was not comforted on this earth, but he had the greater comfort. The last thing he said to me as I was on my way to prison for the last time was, 'Son, I won't see you anymore. I'm soon going to be with your mother and we're going to continue to pray for you . . . .'

"Not long after that he died and I know he came in contact with the Lord Jesus and I can imagine what the Lord Jesus might have said to him: 'John, you have been through a long, dreary, bitter ordeal with that boy of yours, but you loved him and you kept the faith. Now they don't make prison walls high enough nor bars strong enough to keep Me out. You just look down and I'm going to show you a miracle!' And He came into my dungeon cell. I was skin and bones, wasted away under torture. Nothing left in me but the will to hate everybody and everything. Jesus came into my dungeon in person . . . I saw Him. He never said a word to me. His lips were silent. He stood above me, this old wreck, skin and bone, this skeleton poisoned with hate. He stood above me and looked down into my face and drew my eyes which were sunken way back in my head in black sockets. He looked down into my eyes and He just pulled all that poison right out of me with His own eyes . . . In a few moments He just stood there and healed my conscience and gave me a new one. He did it all with the medicine of love."

The rest of the Starr Daily story of God's power in redemption is history. His years of service for prison reform and his witness to his Living Lord have been a blessing and an inspiration around the earth. No one can refute God's miracle in this man. What an answer to his father's prayers!

Starr Daily's father kept the faith because his faith was in *God,* he kept unbroken love for a wayward son, because he had a love that was not dependent upon response. This faith opened the door to the secret of God-love.

To enter into fellowship with God in such love one must accept the application of that love in every relationship. The worse the situation the more the love required. This is the story of the Cross. The more hate they hurled at Jesus the greater the love He released. This is the revelation of the love of God. This is the love we receive and the love which we are asked to show to others.

This love means concern for the needs and sorrows of others but it is a love of concern without anxiety. Tagore, the great Indian poet said. "The end of anxiety is the beginning of being." As Christians we can add that the end of anxiety is the beginning of faith in the God of love who promised us through Jesus Christ that He would meet our every need, no matter how great, no matter how small. We have the *now* only, God will care for the past if we let Him, and He goes with us and our families into the future.

No matter what our problems we look to God's Word as true for our situation.

"God is love; he who dwells in love is dwelling in God, and God in him. . . . There is no room for fear in love; perfect love banishes fear" (I John 4:16, 18, NEB). "The Lord is near: have no anxiety, but in everything make your requests known to God in prayer and petition with thanksgiving. Then the peace of God, which is beyond our utmost understanding, will keep guard over your hearts and your thoughts, in Christ Jesus" (Philippians 4:6, 7, NEB). It seems sometimes that these words of God were written especially for parents of teen-agers today.

To help in the daily discipline of God's love keep these words before you (on your mirror or on your kitchen bulletin board):

Love is patient;
Love is kind and envies no one.
Love is never boastful, nor conceited, nor rude;
    never selfish, not quick to take offence.
Love keeps no score of wrongs;
    does not gloat over other men's sins,
    but delights in the truth.
There is nothing love cannot face
    there is no limit to its faith, its hope, its endurance.
Love will never come to an end.

                    (I Corinthians 13:4-8, NEB)

BIBLIOGRAPHY

Bier, Wm. C., *The Adolescent: His Search for Understanding*, New York, Fordham University Press, 1963.

Drakeford, John W., *The Home: Laboratory of Life*, Nashville, Broadman Press, 1965.

Duvall, Evelyn M., and others, *The Church Looks at Family Life*, Nashville, Broadman Press, 1964.

Ellzey, W. Clark, *Preparing Your Children for Marriage*, New York, Association Press, 1964.

Fromm, Erich, *The Art of Loving*, New York, Harper & Row, 1956. (Bantam Book).

Fromme, Allan, *The Ability to Love*, New York, Farrar, Straus and Giroux, 1965.

Howe, Reuel L., *The Creative Years*, New York, Seabury Press. 1958.
————, *Herein is Love*, Valley Forge, Pa., Judson Press, 1961.

Hulme, Wm. E., *The Pastoral Care of Families*, Nashville, Abingdon Press, 1962.

Jung, C. G., *The Undiscovered Self*, Boston, Little Brown and Co., 1958. (Mentor Book, 1959)

Koonce, Ray., *Understanding Your Teen-agers*, Nashville, Broadman Press, 1965.

Loomis, Earl S. Jr., M.D., *The Self in Pilgrimage*, New York, Harper and Row, 1960.

Mace, David R., *Success in Marriage*, Nashville, Abingdon Press, 1958.

Marney, Carlyle, *Dangerous Fathers, Problem Mothers, and Terrible Teens*, Nashville, Abingdon Press, 1958.

Sherrill, Lewis J., *The Struggle of the Soul*, New York, The Macmillan Co., 1952.

Smith, Sally Liberman, *Nobody Said It's Easy*, New York, The Macmillan Co., 1965.

Stein, Robert, Editor, *Why Young Mothers Feel Trapped*, New York, Trident Press, 1965.

Sweazy, George E., *In Holy Marriage*, New York, Harper and Row, 1966.

Trueblood, Elton and Pauline, *The Recovery of Family Life*, New York, Harper and Row, 1953.

Webb, Lance, *Discovring Love*, Nashville, Abingdon Press, 1959.

White, Patricia and Christine, *To Love is to Grow*, Nashville, Abingdon Press, 1962.

Winter, Gibson, *Love and Conflict*: The New Pattern in Family Life, New York: Doubleday and Co., Dolphin Books, 1958.

Wood, Leland Foster, *How Love Grows in Marriage*, Manhasset, N.Y., Channel Press, 1950.

Wynn, John Charles, *How Christian Parents Face Family Problems*, Philadelphia, Westminster Press, 1955.

————, *Pastoral Ministry to Families*, Philadelphia, Westminster Press, 1957.